this is a gift for the beautiful:

FACETS OF GRIEF© ▼ *A creative approach to grief*

What Others are Saying

"Thank you for this workshop!! I thought I was healing on my own but I wasn't! This has really helped me so much. Thank you for taking your hard things and turning them into something beautiful."
- Christina

"I LOVE this workshop and every week hits me."
-Alison

"Thank you so much for putting my emotions down in black and white. It helps to pinpoint what seems foggy in my head at times."
- Meghann

"This workshop has helped me put my feelings down on paper, love, anger, tears, heartache and learn to own them and to know its okay to feel like the way we do."
-Sonya

"This has given me a outlet to express my grief instead of holding it all in."
- Jamie

"I actually find myself going back to old workshops and re-tweaking them. It's really therapeutic!"
- Val

"It helps to connect with others, to try new things, to explore a bit deeper into my heart and I find artistic creativity is good for that."
- Faith

4

Facets of Grief

A creative workbook for grieving mothers

by Franchesca Cox

FACETS OF GRIEF© ▼ *A creative approach to grief*

Table of Contents

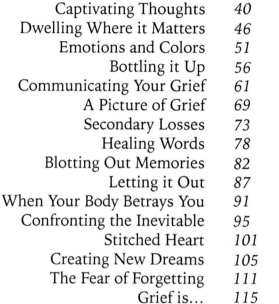

FACETS OF GRIEF© ▼ *A creative approach to grief*

Welcome to Facets of Grief. I invite you to lay your mask down. Here, you can be just you. Clear eyes, open heart. You don't need to hide behind a shield or pretend to have it altogether. You also don't need to apologize for your tears, your anger, your apathy in life, your feelings.

Grief is messy. And this is one place you won't need any explanations for just how messy it is.

These pages you hold in your hands have been three years in the making, and is evidence of the aftermath that happens when grief and love collide. This is a creative workshop, but like any sensible art teacher, I have an obligation to admit that creativity is born of experience and necessity, not talent. You have survived the impossible. You are living a nightmare. You have done the hard part. This part - the living through the aftermath - is the second hardest thing you will ever do.

If at any time you simply cannot go through with a prompt or finish a task in the workshop, step back, take a breath and listen to your heart. Grief is some of the hardest work you will ever do.

Grief is the price we pay for love and it is one we pay so willingly.

But grief is also **work**.

Whether two weeks or twenty years has gone by, grief has a way of finding a place and time in your life to summon your full attention. It demands to be felt. Because love is forever, so is grief.

This workshop is not about finding a way out of grief, but a healthy way into it.

Every prompt has been specifically designed to help you actively, intentionally work through your grief. It is designed to help you take control, recognize *your* grief patterns, new loves, tastes, and basic humanity that feels charred in the aftermath of losing a child. It includes hands-on and practical applications including art therapy, art journaling, basic journaling, self-care ideas, affirmations, words of encouragement and much more.

You might be two months or twenty years into your grief, but as we all know, grief has a way of rising up at the most unexpected moment. Grief leaves no one unscathed, and is no more predictable than the weather.

Facets of Grief is a workshop that allows you to dive into all stages of grief, specific to that of losing a child.

Facets of Grief is about finding your breath again in this life, finding what makes you inhale love, and ready to exhale all that does not serve you in your healing process. It honors your timeline, and realizes that each situation is as unique as fingerprints. No two stories - in spite of any parallels - are the same. This workshop is personal. It is not about achieving the same outcome for each person, but guiding you toward a path of intentional living, however that might look to you. It is also a workshop that is centered around learning to love yourself, care for yourself and trust yourself again. Loss cripples so much more than what lets on outwardly, and ripples into our lives infinitely.

My hope in writing this creative workbook is to help you discover new tools or guide you to some old and forgotten ones along the way. May these creative tools help you assess, express and discover what makes your soul come alive in spite of it all. You, your story, your love and your pain are worth it all.

How to Use this Book

There are 37 prompts altogether. Each prompt has four* parts:

Discussion

Application

Self-Care

Journaling pages

There are bonus coloring pages scattered throughout the workbook.

It is recommend to give each prompt at least 1-2 weeks to soak in. Find a quiet, safe space to do this. Free yourself of expectations, judgments, criticism and anything that attempts to box in your grief or tie it up in a pretty little bow. Light some candles, diffuse some oils, play some relaxing music. This is a creative space that follows only one rule.

Listen to your heart.

If a prompt isn't serving you, it isn't meant for you. Skip over it. Make a note of it, date it and move on. Revisit these prompts from time to time. Grief evolves as time gives us a space to adapt. Things that might derail you today might serve you tomorrow. And vice versa.

Take heart. You may feel utterly alone but let this book serve as a testament that there are thousands upon thousands of mother hearts around the world that get it.

Identity

Art Therapy Prompt 1

Losing my daughter came with a lot of collateral damage, as I like to call it. Losses that were direct results of my daughter's death. They ALL took me by surprise. Because when you lose your child, without knowing it you expect your world around to cater to your grief. You naively believe the world will suddenly stop spinning on it's axis, so that daylight never shines on this desolate land you've been thrust into. Light feels like betrayal to this barren wasteland.

Collateral damage includes the loss of friends (ones I made, and the ones I lost), relationship changes and growth, and so much more. The one that shook me to the core though, and had a direct impact on my interaction with friends and relationships was my identity. Looking in the mirror was like looking at a stranger. It's like I was trying to grow to fit in this new person's skin that no longer felt natural or familiar. I no longer recognized the new me. She felt broken, isolated, forgotten, and eternally sad. Just a few months prior, if I was introducing myself my elevator speech would have rolled off my tongue about a young girl in her early twenties full of ideas and dreams of art school, graduate school, and the opportunity I was toying with to work in an art gallery in Midtown who would have sent me to New York City four times a year. The world was my oyster.

Until it wasn't.

I was jolted into this surreal yet very real new reality where I didn't felt I belonged anymore. I began to cloak a lot of what was really going on because most people could not handle what was really left behind. Shards. Brokenness.

Anger. A massive disappointment in the way our society treats grief. And this longing to get over this unbelievable weight of it all, but not "get over it", if you know what I mean. I was still someone's daughter, wife, daughter-in-law, teacher, friend, acquaintance, co-worker. But my elevator speech would not want to tell you about any of those, it would want to instantly pour out the biggest and grandest thing that has ever happened to me. I AM a mother. That was the only thing going through my mind at all times.

I clumsily waffled my way through the dialog with strangers for years trying to find the "appropriate" way to tell them I was a mother, but not to any little person that they could see.

No, I was none of these things or roles exclusively. Everything had changed, along with how I perceived myself, but maybe more importantly how I felt the rest of the world perceived me. I wanted them to remember my pain, in spite the days and weeks and months taking me further and further away from the point of no return. It felt completely unnatural the way the world continued to spin. In spite of mine going to pieces.

If I'd had enough courage, I might have ordered a shirt or cap that stated "My baby died". There was a very, very good reason I wasn't the person others, or even I could recognize anymore.

FACETS OF GRIEF© ▼ *A creative approach to grief*

APPLICATION

What would your name tag be? What do you see yourself as? A mother? A bereaved mother? Broken? Lost? Would it be a docile definition or more aggressive? Would yours be the same for both parties (family/friends and the rest of the world)? How intimately is your loss weaved into your identity at the moment? Make a name badge - or badges - you may identify with more than one at the moment. Write it out on a piece of paper, or better yet, a blank T-shirt or cap. You don't necessarily have to wear it, but OWN - and be apologetic about where your heart is. Grief is messy and uncomfortable at best. Start unraveling and take heart. This will not be the only badge you will ever wear again.

BADGE

Use the badges on the next page to explore your identity in grief.

SELF-CARE

Go on a hike, nature walk, walk around your neighborhood or nearby lake. Treat yourself to an outdoor retreat from the world. Breathe in the fresh air, exhale any tightness, tenseness and exhaustion you might be holding in.

BADGE

BADGE

BADGE

BADGE

BADGE

BADGE

FACETS OF GRIEF© ▼ *A creative approach to grief*

I didn't expect to lose so much of myself when I lost you. I'll spend the rest of my life learning who I've become and wondering who you would have been.

FACETS OF GRIEF© ▼ *A creative approach to grief*

....

....

....

....

....

....

....

....

....

....

....

....

....

....

....

....

....

....

....

....

FACETS OF GRIEF© ▼ *A creative approach to grief*

Create

Art Therapy Prompt 2

There is power in making this impossible thing called grief tangible, visible. Grief is an elephant in every room in your life, and yet it is something no one can see, or feel - but you. The concept of nearly every exercise in this workshop is to help you visualize grief and work through it. Sort it out like puzzle pieces. A puzzle you can pick and drop at your own convenience. At your own timetable. At your own pace.

There are a couple of ways to make this practical. One would be to make a journal designated for each of the prompts in this book. Almost all of them can be done through solely writing, although you will be offered with different and often more creative ways to tackle each prompt.

Another is to make an *art journal*.

Art journaling is a colorful way to illustrate your thoughts, and express your grief. Sometimes writing alone doesn't cut it. Sometimes you need the messiness, the openness and the adventure that an art journal provides.

The thought of an art journal might seem daunting for you if you don't feel like you are a creative or crafty person, but the truth is art journaling has little to do with talent, and everything to do with exploring and accepting it as a process piece rather than a finished one. Creating an art journal is not about making a beautiful masterpiece in the end; in this case, it is about making your grief tangible and giving your heart a voice. And while it does not have to be beautiful or massively creative, I can almost promise you that you will surprise your own self.

How to Make an Art Journal

What you will need:

an old book, notebook or journal

Supplies worth exploring:

paints, cut out words and letters from magazines, tissue paper, stickers, mod podge, glue sticks, stamps, permanent markers, glitter and photographs

To begin creating an art journaling page, take a piece of paper (pretty much any paper will do) and cut it out the size of the art journal pages. Paste it on each side of an individual page from the art journal, or several for added thickness and texture. Each page is a work in progress and can be as different from the rest of the art journal as you wish. Embrace diversity, as grief can be extremely diverse and unpredictable from day to day.

In case you are a visual learner and would like to see some samples from past students, you can visit facetsofgrief.com and click on the "Gallery" link at the top of the page or simply google "art journal" into your search engine, which will render you literally thousands of ideas! Find what speaks to your soul. It might be a play with words, a certain color or colors, playing with texture, or creating a space to pour your words into. Think of items you have around your home already and find a place to begin your heart work. Above all else, be gentle on yourself. Grief is some of the hardest work you will ever do in your life.

♡♡ APPLICATION

On the first page at the top of your journal write down what you wrote for your badge - where you are today. At the bottom of the page, write what you hope to gain from this workbook.

Is it finding happiness again? Being "okay"? Laughing without guilt? Releasing anger? Forgiving yourself or someone else? Acceptance? Peace? Courage? Something else altogether?

Next, consider what will happen between now and then.

The experience, acts of courage on your part, relationships, revelations, heart work and immense grief work that will take place. I hardly believe that it has anything to do with time. *Time is the vessel that carries us from one heart place to another but in and of itself bears no healing properties.* We get to decide whether or not to listen to our heart, and tune into grief to know when it is time to guide our hearts in a new direction. Never rush and respect the mantra of grief. Grief takes her time as she carries your heart from "stage" to "stage" in no particular order.

SELF-CARE

Sip on tea or your favorite warm drink in a fancy tea cup or favorite mug. Chamomile, peppermint, chai and citrus are wonderful tea flavors for resting your heart and mind, as well as finding new strengths.

It wasn't about getting back what she lost. It was about trying to exist in a world that no longer felt like home.

··

··

··

··

··

··

··

··

··

··

··

··

··

··

··

··

··

··

··

FACETS OF GRIEF© ▼ *A creative approach to grief*

FACETS OF GRIEF© ▼ *A creative approach to grief*

Unmasking Grief

ART THERAPY PROMPT 3

I don't know when it started exactly, but the mask went up pretty fast. It became painfully obvious that after a few weeks of burying our baby girl, almost everyone around me was ready to resume the life that I was having a hard time loving again. The reality that this was *my* grief, and mine alone (aside from my husband) was setting in. There was a gnawing feeling that I was being left behind and perhaps I was stuck somewhere unhealthy. No one set out to intentionally make me feel any of this, but I still felt utterly and completely alone. As time passed, I mastered the art of pretension. I sat through mind-numbing conversations about things I could not possibly care about, as long as I could bear, but lost a significant amount of friends anyway. The pain dripped from my eyes, and it came out anyway. The mask served many purposes, survival being one of them, but hindered me too.

I became frustrated with this mask that was feeling more and more uncomfortable by the minute, which was defeating the purpose of wearing it in the first place.

Someone finally told me to embrace my grief. That was probably the best advice I was ever given - because as I shared earlier even in my feeble attempt to shadow my real pain, it bled out anyway. Embracing it was going to be painful but it was the best thing I did for myself those first few years. I can't say it saved relationships that were past saving, but it did for the first time since my loss help me focus on what my heart needed (which over time was much more than a mask), clarified what self-care looked like, why it was more than new-age lingo and vital to healing.

It helped me confront all the wild and unpredictable emotions of grief head-on. And while even my husband did not understand the roller coaster I was facing without him many times, grieving openly and honestly for the first time liberated me toward my first steps of healing.

Do you find yourself wearing a mask in public? Do you feel like it is helping you, or hindering you? Maybe a little bit of both, depending on where you are or who you are with? Embrace your answer. There is no right or wrong. Consider unmasking your grief, and leaning into it.

It's all about those baby steps.

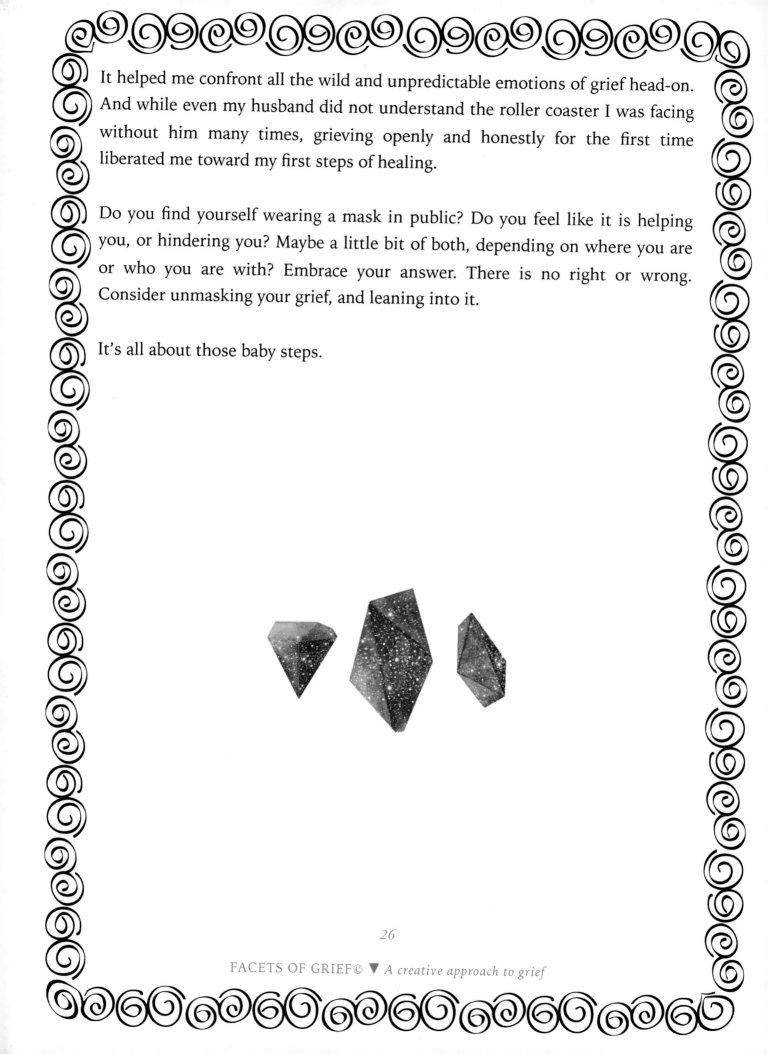

APPLICATION

Put together a Grief Survival Kit. Pick things around your home that symbolize the emotions you feel frequently in new grief, such as anger, confusion, sadness, loneliness, hopelessness, longing. Some ideas for items: key, dice, rubber band, eraser, paper clip, lock, piece of twine, stone, seashells, feathers, beads, crystals, a knotted rope, handkerchief, tea light candle and tangled string to name a few.

Keep them in a little knapsack in your purse, car or somewhere easy to find. When you are feeling the waves of grief higher than usual, reach for the item you've associated with the emotion you are presently feeling. Hold it close, and breathe through your grief with intentional, deep breaths. Breathing in your emotion, validating it and exhaling love. Validating each emotion will begin to feel more natural.

If you can intentionally grieve and be honest with yourself about where you stand in grief, you have made tremendous progress.

Write about each item in your art journal, or in the note pages provided at the end of this section. Describe why you chose what you did.

 SELF-CARE

Keep a small notepad handy or make good use of your phone's reminder apps to help your tired mind remember important dates and appointments. Grief has a way of clouding the mind and crippling our memory.

Under her mask were the secret scars of life and death. Under her mask was someone she was becoming. Under her mask was someone she didn't recognize, but welcomed anyway.

FACETS OF GRIEF© ▼ *A creative approach to grief*

29

Broken Glass

Art Therapy Prompt 4

It is impossible enough to think about getting through another day without your child, especially in the beginning of grief. Grief begins to manifest it's endless and permanent mark in your life as the days turn into weeks and the weeks into months and the months into years. To make matters worse, triggers are just about everywhere you go. What used to be a casual trip to the store has turned into a wasteland saturated with unsuspecting landmines of what could have, would have and should have been.

It is as if you are walking on a floor completely covered in shards of broken glass. And it hurts - no matter where you go, and what you do. Somehow everything little and big thing takes you back.

It becomes harder and harder to explain this experience to the world around you as time goes on. For example, why the baby section doesn't get easier to pass by. Or why baby showers, pregnancy announcements and all sorts of longed-for milestones in a child's life carry a sting. Or why holding a new baby, even years later, brings both tears of joy and sorrow. The uneasiness is sometimes accompanied by guilt, and it all gets so complicated, so fast.

As time goes by though, it seems like some triggers don't fade with time. They are able to take you back to that room, that moment, that place in a split second. As you feel ready, it is important to begin to equip yourself with some truths when this happens. Guard you heart, and each time these triggers take you back anyway, let them. It's what makes you human. Resisting triggers prematurely may only hinder your progression through grief. As you reel back into a calmer state of mind, consider the trigger. What emotions were stirred? Was guilt, regret or anger involved? Sadness and longing? Begin to wrap you heart with some gentle truths.

You are grieving deeply because you loved deeply. Grief is an incredibly personal experience and will change you to the core, forever. Honor this truth. Breathe into it. Be patient with yourself. At the heart of all this hurt, is the love for the one you are living without. Never forget that.

What are your triggers? Is there one or two that stand out from the rest? How do you approach these situations? Is it unbearable to think about managing or diffusing your reaction to them right now? If so, that is okay! This exercise below is only to help you recognize them. Any further steps you take all depend on your heart, and yours alone.

♡ APPLICATION

List your triggers. You might even collage pictures of them, with cutouts from magazines and newspapers. Continue to paste images that symbolize your triggers in your art journal until the sting begins losing it's power. Paint over them, scribble over them, write over them.

Conquer them

Begin writing some truths to guard your heart for the next trigger attack. What truths can you breathe into your heart and soul to nurture your heart through one your trigger attacks? How can you give your heart a space to grieve, while maintaining your ground?

It is okay to feel hurt, alone, hopeless, forgotten, jealous, angry - you fill in the blank. Our grief is as unique as as our thumbprints. The goal is to recognize which situations bring these feelings to the surface and take control of the situation rather than the situation ambush us. This process happens organically if you allow yourself to with intention and patience with yourself.

♡ SELF-CARE

Learn to say no. It might be totally out of your comfort zone, but if there was ever a time to give into selfishness, it would be now. Take this time to reflect on your feelings, the darkness that might be flooding your life and even the light trying to break through. You need this time to adjust to the aftermath of grief. Be okay with letting the right people down. As Dr. Seuss once said, "Those who mind don't matter and those who matter don't mind."

While the world felt like a landmine of reminders and triggers, she decided her mind would be her fortress. The one thing, maybe the only thing in all this disaster, she could control.

FACETS OF GRIEF© ▼ *A creative approach to grief*

FACETS OF GRIEF© ▼ *A creative approach to grief*

The Searching

Art Therapy Prompt 5

I don't know how it even started but right after she died, I would constantly be staring at the clouds. I probably looked ten different kinds of crazy, but I didn't care. I just remember lots of puffy cotton ball clouds those days. It was always dreadfully sunny, when all I felt was a never-ending rainstorm going on in my heart. I became obsessed with finding messages through heart-shaped clouds, or spotting butterflies, and small birds perched on power lines. I saw her in the small children at the park, her empty chair at our dinner table, and in fuchsia things everywhere I went. Sunsets had an entirely new significance and brought me to tears many times, especially the ones where pinks and purples danced across the sky. I still am mesmerized by sunsets and it all goes back to her. I like to think she helps paint that beautiful mess in the sky.

I had these symbols to remember her by, and it became an obsession of mine to find her everywhere I went. In the beginning it felt like everything was a reminder of her existence and a reminder of our loss, but as time went on it felt as though time had swallowed her up completely, with no ripples or undertows to validate how unnatural it was for a child to die. Her death did not send the universe into catastrophe, as it had my entire life. Finding these symbols and colors in my surroundings helped me to honor her short life in a tangible way.

♡♡ APPLICATION

Is there something you collect to remember your loved one by? Or is there something that instantly makes you think of them like a *scent or place*? Write about these symbols and any special places in your home. Additionally, you can paste photographs of this area in your home, as this space could potentially evolve over time.

♥ SELF-CARE

Take five minutes out of your day to sit in complete silence. Turn off electronic devices if possible. Release yourself of any obligations for just five minutes. Give yourself permission to focus on nothing else but your breath. Start your exercise by releasing any excess tension throughout your jaw, face and wrists. Relax your shoulders. Rest in a comfortable sitting position with your palms facing up on your thighs or knees. Simply let yourself be. Listen to each natural breath you take. After a few breathes, take it deeper if you can. Take a deep breathe and notice the way it affects your chest, lungs and your diaphragm. Hold it for 2-3 seconds and slowly exhale. Close your eyes and repeat this breathing exercise 3-5 times. Open your eyes. Take time to focus your breathing when you find yourself in a stressful situation. You might only have a few seconds, but refocusing your energy on your core essentials puts everything back into a healthy perspective.

I look for you everywhere. The twinkle in the stars, the sway of the trees, the whispers in the wind, the reflections in the water, the sunrising and the sunset. And I will keep looking.

FACETS OF GRIEF© ▼ *A creative approach to grief*

FACETS OF GRIEF© ▼ *A creative approach to grief*

Captivating Thoughts

Art Therapy Prompt 6

Have you ever just been standing, sitting, eating simply walking in public and suddenly burst into tears? Yea, me too. In fact, it happened all the time in the beginning, which is a lot of the reason I dreaded and often avoided going out unnecessarily. It was frustrating how little control I had over my emotions. There were dark memories that haunted me, but most of the time it was absolutely nothing that sent me spiraling into a puddle of tears.

My. Heart. Was. Broken.

I was having a lunch date with a fellow loss mom and friend a few weeks after we lost Jenna, and as we were talking I began suddenly crying. As I gathered myself she lent me words that I will never forget - and to be quite honest they stung a little too. It was the first time someone didn't try to respond instantly with compassion. It was a new response to this mess I had suddenly become, and it was equal parts refreshing and hurtful, I will admit. She told me in so many words that I needed to find a way to control my mind. Granted, if that had come from anyone besides a bereaved mother, I would not have given those words a second thought. In fact I might never have spoken to them again.

But here she was, a loss mom herself, and I know she was trying to help me. At the time, I can remember soaking in those words because she obviously had experience in the department of grief but I, myself, could not ever imagine putting these unpredictable emotions into any type of subjection. I was a mess everywhere I went. Everything little thing reminded me of Jenna. It was ridiculous how fervent and effortlessly grief crept into every caveat of my life and surroundings.

Is it even possible to practice mind control in the grief that involves losing a child? I believe it is entirely possible over time, but you have to learn to recognize the pattern that your mind works in. And I say "learn" because most of the time it won't be something that will come naturally or right away. After experiencing the loss of a child, we become more in tune with our mind and body, more intimately than ever before. It's as if the mute button on our emotions has been ripped off and all we can hear, see, touch, smell, taste is our pain. We know the way grief smells, and the waves that wash over us, we know how heavy they feel. We hear grief whisper on our hearts throughout the day, of all the little and big ways we're missing out. We have become well-acquainted with visible pain that meets us in the mirror each morning, and we can taste it because nothing else tastes the same. The world around you has become muted and the only things that speak to you are things that help you make sense of this intense pain.

Lean into the pain, and let is wash over you. Grief is the price we pay for love and it is one we pay so willingly. As you let grief have her way in your life, over time you will start to hear that pain screaming at the highest decibel begin to dwindle down to a low roar. It won't hurt any less, but you will become familiar with your grief patterns and learn to harness control over situations that before were unavoidable inward catastrophes.

One thing I wished this friend would have told me was to let it happen in my own time. Maybe she knew that I would realize over time that I could never rush this process of mind control, but I am here, laying a plea of caution in this arena, just in case.

Grief is messy. So let it be as messy as it needs to be for as long as it needs to be. But you must know, that inside you is not only the power to love, to grieve but also to heal.

Grief demands to be felt before it can be harnessed.

APPLICATION

Over time you will learn how to reel your mind back into a healthier place when triggers take a jab at your heart. If you know you cannot a trigger happy place or situation, equip yourself with some truths mentioned earlier. It might be a verse you cling to, a mantra you resonate with, a breathing exercise to to help you focus on your diaphragm breathing instead of crying. You may even carry your *Grief Survival Kit* (Prompt 3) with you to give you something to hold onto. It can be anything. The worst thing you can do is to enter these situations unguarded.

I cannot count the number of times I would have to excuse myself and cry it out in a closet or bathroom before joining a crowd again. Crowds were difficult to stay in, even (especially?) if they were friends and family. Practicing mind control over time helped me to accept whatever I was feeling and over time redistribute those intense feelings into something else like deep breathing, taking a walk, making a mental to-do list, diving into a conversation I could actually care nothing about (distraction and class at it's finest!), or even offering to do the dishes at social functions - which provided me a safe space to fall apart without leaving.

In what ways can you practice mind control when your natural reaction would be to fall apart? During a moment of bravery, hope or inspiration write down a mantra, a distracting idea or a truth to yourself. **What do you wish you could remember or focus on in those moments of falling apart?** Write it out in colorful, vibrant markers or crayons. **Be bold.** You are the only one that holds the key to opening up your heart again.

SELF-CARE

Ask for help. Be specific. Where do you feel you could use a little support? Take your friends and family up on their kind offers to assist you. Often, they have no idea what you need. As time moves forward you realize exactly what your heart needs. Speak out in courage.

She sat in darkness because it was the only place that felt like home anymore. Yes, the darkness was haunted with memories and often dangerous to walk alone, but it understood her brokenness and gave her a place to ask hard questions.

....

....

....

....

....

....

....

....

....

....

....

....

....

....

....

....

....

....

FACETS OF GRIEF© ▼ *A creative approach to grief*

Dwelling Where it Matters

ART THERAPY PROMPT 7

For the longest time I battled with placing my daughter, mentally, in a good place after she died. I didn't think she was sad, or hurting or anything like that. I believed and still believe she went to Heaven, but it haunted me that I could not mentally "put" her there. It bothered me. I kept visualizing, and having this nightmare (though it would take me by surprise all while I was awake too) of those last moments holding her struggling, dying body. I hated remembering her this way, because she was so much more than a sick baby. She was and *is* more than my dead baby. She was beautiful. She was our first. She was so wanted. She is so incredibly loved.

She had personality. And spunk. And tight ringlets of dark hair all over her little head. She looked like me.

She was all those good things, and more.

Something I talked to my pastor's wife was this occurring daymare. She encouraged me to picture her in a positive light and to be detailed about it. She made this story of how she pictured her now. She said,"I see her riding around on a tricycle on the street of gold, in a red polka dot dress with pig tails. And no doubt Grandpa is right there with her."

It helped. This detailed and wild imaginative story to tell myself. Placing her out of that dark memory, and placing her beautiful face in a wonderful and happy place. It moved my grief to a much less confusing place to say the least. I believed in Heaven and the whole shebang, but nothing about losing a child is easy, and this part of the struggle surprised me. And, obviously, I have no earthly idea what Heaven is really like, but it helped to challenge these awful memories with hopes that she is not only healthy, but a thriving and happy child doing childish, happy things. It also helped to read the parts of Revelations that describe Heaven. I wanted to know every detail of where I believe my daughter is.

♡♡ APPLICATION

In a page in your art journal, list the emotions you can think of that have really manifested in your grief since your loss. Some common ones are depression, isolation, anger, peace, loneliness, sadness, jealousy, bitterness, denial, gratitude, indifference.

After listening them in your journal begin thinking about what color instantly comes to mind when you feel this emotion. It should not take much time to associate this emotion with a color. Some colors can be used twice or even involve a mix or 2 or more colors. Why do you think these colors you picked are associated with these emotions? In the future, reference this emotion color guide and try to use these colors for future prompts. For prompts that stimulate anger or bitterness use the associated colors, and for prompts that make you feel gratitude or a bit of acceptance or peace use the appropriate colors. It should be an interesting way to color coordinate your grief and grief "journey" throughout your art journal.

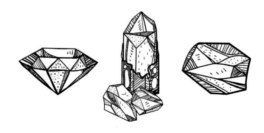

♡ SELF-CARE

It is important to be conscious of your health, even in your grief. It might feel like the least important matter when you are trying to just survive. One of the easiest ways you can maintain your health is to stay hydrated. Aim to drink the eight glasses a day, and maybe even more. Fill an ice tray with fresh or frozen fruit and then fill to the brim with water. In a few hours drop these beauties into a glass of water to enjoy fresh fruit-infused water.

Grief could transcend the present moment, invade each of her five senses, overcome impossible measures and take her right back to where it all started. Grief was the time traveling machine she had always thought impossible.

FACETS OF GRIEF© ▼ *A creative approach to grief*

....

....

....

....

....

....

....

....

....

....

....

....

....

....

....

....

....

....

....

....

FACETS OF GRIEF© ▼ *A creative approach to grief*

Emotions & Colors

ART THERAPY PROMPT 8

I feel as though grief aged me. Grief taught me so much about myself that I doubt I would have discovered any other way. I can't say that it makes it worth it, but it does make this grief interesting, to say the least. It's as if everything rode right on the surface and it was clearer than ever what my heart needed and demanded at times. Space. Music. Clarity. Something to break or punch. A shoulder to cry on. A journal. A visit to the cemetery. A beach visit. A friend for distraction. A friend to cry to. At times I felt like I needed vodka or something to numb the pain. I never had to guess, because grief was a teacher and I was soaking it up, not aware that I was actually learning something about myself during these harsh months, and years.

I found a concept long after our loss, that I wish I would have known about when we lost her. I believe it would have been helpful to put a pattern or visual to my grief. While grief rode on the surface of my heart and life, I could hardly predict which direction I would be headed next. Having a color to associate would have helped validate these emotions - which is often such a hard thing to do - especially ones like anger, depression, bitterness, jealousy, etc. It involves a little bit of color therapy, but more or less associating your emotion with a color. It is interesting that different colors mean different things for everyone.

♡ APPLICATION

Challenge the bad memories with thoughts worth dwelling on. Write a list. If you lost your child early on you can write about your pregnancy, the cravings you had, baby showers, hearing their heart beat for the first time and buying their first outfit. If you lost a baby, down some things that made them smile, their sweet baby scent, holding them for the first time, the meaning behind their name.

If you have lost a child or an adult child, search your memory and take charge of those bad memories by taking some time to write down the best times you spent together, moments they made you especially proud, their accomplishments, their hopes and dreams and funny, sweet or memorable things they said. Their eyes, their smile, the way they talked and walked. Their goofy personalities, their laugh, their favorite sports team or pair of shoes. While these all serve as painful reminders of what we lost, they can also be forces of light in those dark times. *We have had the privilege of calling these children ours.*

When you are tempted to dwell on a particularly dark or haunting memory, challenge yourself by pulling out this list. Maybe even take some time to make a collage of words, phrases and pictures that bring your list to life in your art journal.

❤ SELF-CARE

If you are able to, take a blanket outside and lay down. Close your eyes and listen to the leaves rustling, the birds singing, the sound of pedestrians and cars rushing in the background. You might be fortunate to live near water. Listen for the waves, the crickets, the sea gulls. Place one hand over your heart and the other over your abdomen. Breathe naturally, inhaling peace and exhaling fatigue. Inhaling love, exhaling fear. Inhaling forgiveness, exhaling anger. Replace these emotions with the ones going on in your own heart.

....

....

....

....

....

....

....

....

....

....

....

....

....

....

....

....

....

....

....

....

....

....

··

··

··

··

··

··

··

··

··

··

··

··

··

··

··

··

··

··

··

55

Bottling it Up

Art Therapy Prompt 9

I don't know when it starts but after a certain point in grief, we all feel it in some degree or another - the urge - sometimes gentle, sometimes not - to move on, to be okay, to get on with life. Your circle of people does not want to see you hurting, and you know this. You also realize how impossible it is to "be okay", to "move on" (where to, exactly!?), to get on with life. So it is natural to find a compromise between both worlds and stuff our pain. We become persuaded that this is the only way to exist. Secretly hurting. Secretly angry. Secretly ill. Secretly and most definitely not okay. All of the time.

This is not an advocacy of entitled or obnoxious behavior(though I have to confess I have let myself slip into this arena early on in my grief), but I do think it can be done in grace, honesty and love. It will not always be socially acceptable to wear your grief openly, but this can open doors for important conversations about the reality of child loss, life after loss. It can also make significant steps toward tearing down the taboo over child loss.

We are hurting.

We are, so often, *not* okay.

We are not alone, yet that is exactly how we feel.

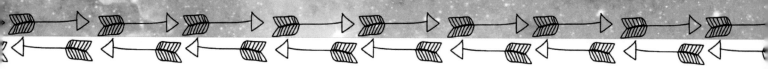

♡♡ APPLICATION

Let's pretend you have a bottle. This bottle is home to all the emotions the rest of the world cannot see or possibly imagine you are feeling. What emotions and feelings live in this bottle? Are they something you feel you *must* internalize? If so, why? Consider why you have hid them from the rest of the world? Have they been tirelessly wrecking havoc on your life? Have they created strain in your relationships? Have they been too heavy to deal with outwardly? Are they safe here? Do you feel they might explode at some point? Is there the possibility that you can show them outwardly?

Fill the bottle with emotions and feelings and thoughts that feel trapped inside of you. You can even use a real life bottle and write on strips of paper.

How could you go about effectively communicating your emotions you are stuffing at the moment? From who are they hidden? Everyone? Significant other? Children? Friends? Sometimes it isn't relationships that shut our emotional lines down, sometimes it is just being exhausted from grief itself. Grief is work. Impossibly-hard-to-describe work. Feeling it. Feeling jarred. Feeling angry. Feeling angry. Feeling bitter. None of these particular emotions are places to dwell, but thinking we can escape them altogether (if they are something you are up bottling up), is pure fantasy. They will be manifested. Feel them. Take control by validating the emotions on an inhale and releasing them with a lot of deep breaths and exhales.

Use this exercise to illustrate the picture of what's going on inside. Take a bucket of courage to do some soul and heart searching.

♡ SELF-CARE

Sit outside with the intention of doing nothing else except watching the sun rise or set.

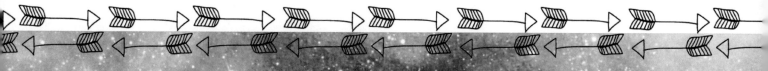

Bottling it up

Grief is not a nuisance, an obstacle or mess that can easily be rectified. It is a way of life.
It is everything you never thought could happen but did anyway.

59

FACETS OF GRIEF© ▼ *A creative approach to grief*

Communicating Your Grief

Art Therapy Prompt 10

In the beginning, and actually for a very long time I believed that I was telling Jenna's story through my own. And I think in some ways I was... *am*. I still talk about her, though not as often and most certainly not to everyone. It's just different. Not a day goes by that I don't think about her in same way or fashion. It took me a long time to realize and accept - and I think that is the key word - that I was and am currently telling my story. *My story*. Totally separate from Jenna's. Intertwined, beautifully and tragically tangled together, but separate nonetheless.

Consider that you have a story to tell too. In fact, every day that you rise to face the music, you are telling a piece of it. To your family, your friends, your co-workers, your neighbors and on and on it goes.

It is a common misfortune in the child loss community that the lines of communication seem to close about our grief and all things related much sooner than we are ready for them to. And then again, are we ever ready? It's impossible to say. But at some point it is vital not only to our survival - but ultimate "THRIVE-al" of life to learn new ways to communicate and tell our story, effectively. It would be a tragedy for us to merely survive this life by the skin of our teeth, when we of all people, have walked and co-existed so intimately with death. To us, life isn't just a gift - it is precious, wildly unpredictable and something we cannot take for granted for very long.

Is it possible to communicate with others about our grief when the doors seem shut? I believe it is. I am certainly no expert, but suffice it to say, I have made my fair share of mistakes of what not to do. In addition, some people I never imagined would "come through", did in a totally beautiful and unexpected way. I believe the number one thing in the matter is understanding that most of the time, it is not that people are shutting out your grief or saying inappropriate things to hurt you on purpose, they are afraid of hurting you even more. They see you cry, hurt and possibly depressed and the last thing they want to do is make it worse. In a similar light, people fear what they do not know. Hurting people are a scary specimen. Think back to your before. Real, physical and emotional grief is a world they cannot relate to, and they don't know what to do with your pain. So they run, they hide, they find excuses, they change the subject. Our grief becomes even more impossible by this desolation.

But take heart. You are not alone, nor will you ever be.

Do some heart work before proceeding and put two things into place to prepare your heart. Come into this thing with the mindset and belief that most people want to help you. Secondly, and this might seem contradictory, but set your expectations low. If you come into this communicating thing expecting next to nothing, nearly everything will be a surprise, in the best way.

There are a few ways that I "communicated" with the outside world during my hardest seasons of grief. One was creating a blog. I should pause long enough to say that I started a blog for me. But as it turned out, before I even knew it, there were people reading diligently along, people I'd never even shared it with. Some probably read out of mere curiosity (and I'm actually good with that -- any time we can help educate society on real, raw grief I think it is usually a good thing), but many because they did not know how to help me. It let them inside my heart and head, without me having to hash it out in person. If you prefer some privacy, you can create a private blog and send a mass email out to those you hope would want to read, and invite them to read it. You get to control your readership that way.

Another thing you can do, is on a special date, like an anniversary or birthday, you can text your circle of people and ask them to do a Random Act of Kindness in your child's memory. It's not expensive and it is something people usually enjoy doing. It can be a fun thing to do together, especially with social media. You can create your own hashtag too, which might inspire others to take part.

When I pregnant Jenna, in our church seven other mamas were also expecting. My baby came first. It was intensely bittersweet, to say the least, to have to witness all these normal births for the next few months. Deliveries, new babies, birth stories, doting grandparents, dedications. I remember the conversations surrounding these new babies. I was desperate to prove to the world that I too, was a new mom. I had stories, good ones, to contribute. In the beginning it was incredibly awkward. They didn't know what to say. Cry? Walk away? Pretend like Jenna was still alive? They probably thought I was insane. I don't blame them. But I needed this. So I kept on. I would contribute when I felt like I could and wanted to. Breast pumping stories, first time meeting the baby, postpartum recovery, etc. Eventually, I think, people got the message. My stories weren't going anywhere. Just like theirs, mine were real. I needed to be validated and heard. I wasn't out to push my grief on anyone, but I was anxious to talk about my child with people. I wanted people to know she was so much more than a tragic ending. She was an incredible child, and we were the lucky ones, to be her parents.

There was one person in particular that shut me down early on, and this one hurt a lot, a lot. She didn't realize she was doing it - in fact she too was hurting so bad that she just bottled it all up and did so because of her own pain but also because she could not imagine making my own grief worse by "bringing it up". Ultimately I confronted her. I was honest and told her that I needed to talk about Jenna. I needed her conversation with me about the whole thing. Things were not white picket fences and daisies after this confrontation, but it was a step in the right direction. It became increasingly obvious that our relationship could never be what it was without us being able to communicate about this elephant in the room. Ugly, pretty and everything in between. Today, I am thankful to say, this relationship is not only salvaged but thriving.

FACETS OF GRIEF© ▼ *A creative approach to grief*

♥ APPLICATION

Too often people come to us right after the loss, and say something like, "please let me know if you need anything."

If only they knew, we hardly know ourselves.

CHALLENGE YOURSELF to walk up to someone that may have said this to you (or not) and start those lines of communication again.

Make it a priority to approach someone you trust. It might be more subtle like asking them to help you reach a goal for charity or run for a cause. Maybe you need to face the elephant in the room. Let them know you need to talk candidly. Preface the conversation by explaining the *sacredness* and *okayness* of tears. Someone wise once told me people are afraid of hurting people. You cry because you love. People mostly need a chance to grow in this area. They want to fix your pain which is a misguided but noble approach to grief. Be specific with them about your needs. We get convinced that we are wearing our grief openly, but the truth is the longer we are in grief the better we get at masking our pain.

Start with quizzing yourself. ***Do you know what you need right now?*** Would you like them to mention your loved one's name? Remember special dates? Visit the cemetery with you? Sit in silence to remember with you? Light a candle? Hold your hand while you get that tattoo? Just listen? Regular coffee dates? We cannot control their reaction, but we can make the first, proactive step in being specific about what we need. If you enter this conversation with little or no expectations, what have you got to lose?

People. Will. Surprise. You.

♥ SELF-CARE

Get grounded this week. There is scientific research that supports the idea that the earth is a wonderful source of energy and vitality. Take your shoes off and let your soles of your feet touch the ground - soil, sand, grass, dirt, pebbles, even concrete. For more information on grounding, check out the book Earthing.

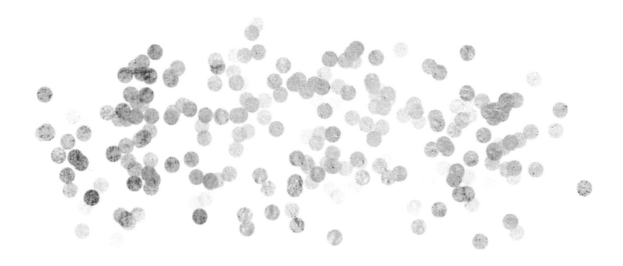

Her grief was as fiery as fire and as unforgiving as a rain storm.

....

....

....

....

....

....

....

....

....

....

....

....

....

....

....

....

....

....

FACETS OF GRIEF© ▼ *A creative approach to grief*

FACETS OF GRIEF© ▼ *A creative approach to grief*

A Picture of Grief

Art Therapy Prompt 11

As a visual person I have wondered for a long time if grief could be illustrated what would it look like? What would the atmosphere feel like? Would it be twilight or midnight? Would the topography be rugged or slippery? Would the stars be visible? Would there be any water or sunlight or rain? I didn't feel like any particular image could do *grief* justice. An awful lot of images on social media capture parts of grief, but none of them encompass every aspect. If you could give grief a landscape what would it look like?

A counselor shared a challenge in a retreat for bereaved parents one summer - to draw a picture of grief using at least two things: mountains and valleys, and a rainbow to symbolize hope [if you could]. You can add anything else in the picture to symbolize grief. There were the expected amounts of *"I'm not an artist"* groans, but the results equally haunting and beautiful.

Are you up for it?

Before you begin:

> 1. Give yourself a 10-15 time limit.
> 2. Use the materials you have on hand. We used a combination of markers, colored pencils and crayons, but again, use what you have on hand.
> 3. And if you can, get a hold of some butcher paper. There is something about intentional, big movements that release emotions [think exercise!]. Newspaper, cardboard and craft paper will work just fine too.

Draw mountains and valleys to illustrate your grief. The rest is up to you. Does a rainbow feel fitting? A rainbow in this scenario is to symbolize hope - nothing more. Is there hope in your life at this very moment?

If you feel stuck, think about a few things like weather, seasons, the earth elements, cliffs, animals, steepness of mountains, topography, and the list could go on. Release yourself from any obligations to create a masterpiece. ***Remember that grief is anything but beautiful.***

SELF-CARE

In the thick of grief, usually the last thing on our mind is taking care of ourselves, and even further down the list is turning our focus to our own health. Guilt, fatigue, indifference and so many other things play a role in this area. If you don't believe it, you deserve it. Begin to think about ways to take care of your body, health, and wellness. It can mean adding color to your plate through fresh fruits and vegetables. It can be drinking water instead of soda. It can be practicing some kind of quiet time in the morning. It can mean going to the gym or exploring a trail in your area.

She had never lived or felt so richly. So vividly. So in tune with her emotions, and how many there could be. She knew now that living deeply came at the highest cost.

··

··

··

··

··

··

··

··

··

··

··

··

··

··

··

··

··

··

FACETS OF GRIEF© ▼ *A creative approach to grief*

Secondary losses

Art Therapy Prompt 12

Secondary losses add salt to an already open wound. They are the losses that are often the most surprising and the ones that magnify grief a thousand fold. Isolated, they might not feel like massive obstacles in our path, but combined with our recent loss, they become a world of grief all on their own.

The most pronounced secondary loss, in our own story, was the innocence during future pregnancies, and somewhat related - the blind trust in my own body to bring a healthy child into this world.

Another secondary loss was the *loss of innocence* with subsequent pregnancies, the absolute wonder and joy that fills the air with the discovery of a new baby on the way. Pregnancy was the second hardest thing I've ever done in my life, because I knew nothing was sure. I battled between ignoring my pregnancy (emotionally) and obsessing over every detail, kick count, ultrasound, potential environmental hazard - you name it. In retrospect, it was obvious that fear drove everything I did and did not do. Unfortunately it also dominated my memories, as I can only recall fragments from that period in my life. It was dreadful and one of my deepest regrets. It is also what spurred my little book, Celebrating Pregnancy Again, into action. It was written while I was pregnant for the third time, with our youngest daughter. I made it my priority to embrace this last pregnancy. While no amount of goodwill could undo what had already been lost and learned, I could take control of where I made my habitation and where I spent my energy- mentally, emotionally and spiritually.

What secondary losses have you experienced? In what ways have you addressed or handled them? Do you feel ready? Writing them down is a huge step in facing these giants.

Sometimes we don't realize just how much has been affected by grief until we take a moment to sit with it a while. Relationships change, your passions suffer, your hopes, dreams, social dynamics, our very own personalities. *It is hard to think of one that that doesn't get even a little bit singed in the fiery of grief.*

Fill out a secondary loss wheel on the next page, or create one in your art journal.

After filling it out, it may surprise you just how much you've lost as a result of your initial loss. Naturally, none of them matter as much, but the perspective of the *collateral damage* on your heart is good to soak in.

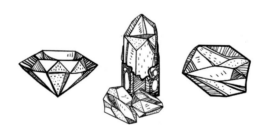

SELF-CARE

Pick up something to read that you normally wouldn't. Something light and fluffy, or something you used to be into. Nothing to do with grief, loss, pain... those topics are off limits for this self-care exercise. Read up on this season's nail polish color, the latest celebrity gossip, or maybe dive into a craft magazine at your local craft store.

Secondary losses

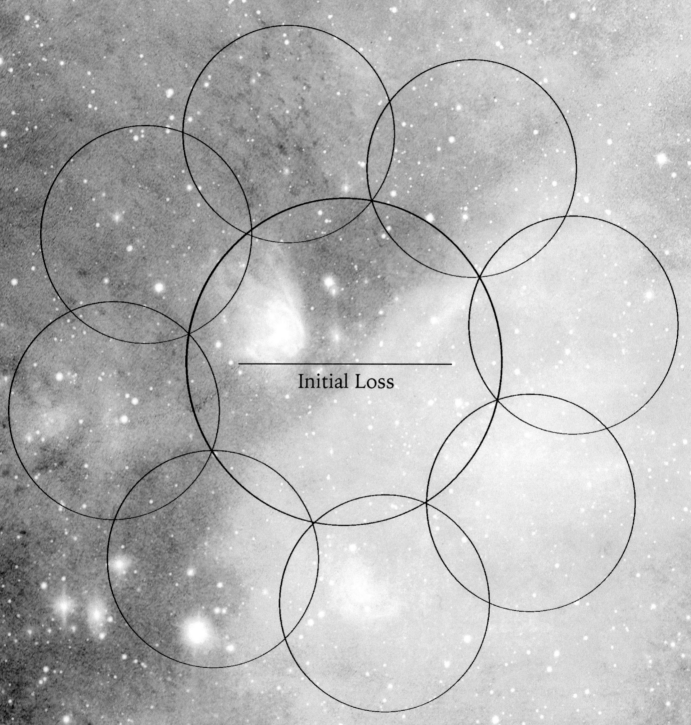

Initial Loss

Perhaps the most surprising thing of all, is that she lost so much of herself in the aftermath.

....

....

....

....

....

....

....

....

....

....

....

....

....

....

....

....

....

....

....

FACETS OF GRIEF© ▼ *A creative approach to grief*

···

···

···

···

···

···

···

···

···

···

···

···

···

···

···

···

···

···

···

Healing Words

Art Therapy Prompt 13

When I was a girl I remember being obsessed with poetry and writing in general, but especially poetry. Years passed and the obsession faded as new interests appeared on the scene, but when we lost Jenna writing became like a lifeline someone threw out to me while drowning. I was instantly drawn into this passion that laid dormant for years. And I held to it for dear life, and spent many sleepless nights just writing. Journaling. Putting feeling to pen and expressing heart songs and tears to paper.

Writing is healing. It draws out what you hide, unveils the mask we get used to wearing, forces us to relinquish the burdens we carry, and most and best of all - validates the pain. Have you used writing in any form to help express your grief?

♡♡ APPLICATION

Your challenge this week is to write a haiku about your grief. If you are not already familiar with it, the haiku is as simple as poetry gets. A haiku is a Japanese form of poetry comprised of 3 verses and 17 syllables - no more, no less. Simplistic in form, the haiku prose is a beautiful way to express the healing process.

First Verse: 5 syllables

Second Verse: 7 syllables

Third Verse: 5 syllables

 SELF-CARE

Pick some flowers for yourself, or if you don't have flowers growing around you treat yourself to a bouquet. There is something about flowers that livens up the atmosphere, and spirits. If possible, make it your goal to always have some flowers in your home. You can even press the flowers to create bookmarks and such with them. And, if you suffer from allergies, artificial flowers can be just as lovely.

- -

- -

- -

- -

- -

- -

- -

- -

- -

- -

- -

- -

- -

- -

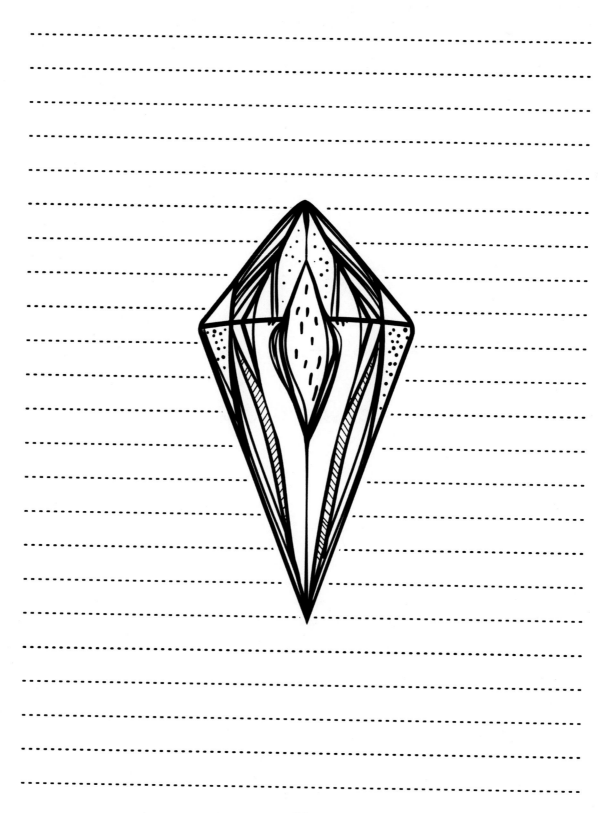

- -

- -

- -

- -

- -

....
....
....
....
....
....
....
....
....
....
....
....
....
....
....
....
....
....
....
....

FACETS OF GRIEF© ▼ *A creative approach to grief*

Blotting Out Memories

ART THERAPY PROMPT 14

It usually doesn't take a whole lot of effort to stir memories that we try to bury under our everyday mask. These are the memories that we often bear alone or share with very few people. The last breaths, the sounds, the smells in the room, the color of the room. The expression of the family members or friends in the room. The clothes we wore, the expressions of the nurses and doctors. The last bath, choosing an outfit for burial.

We have survived the impossible.

The moments that instantly make tears fall sending shock throughout our nervous system and for a split second crippling our ability to do life as we have done it before - seamlessly. It isn't seamless anymore.

We carry memories that are invisible to the rest of the world.

And they aren't just memories, they are thorns that continually pierce open wounds.

As time moves us forward, we find ways to halt these thoughts from taking over our everyday lives, but they don't ever become any less painful. Time lends us the space to adapt to this new normal but true healing can only come when we learn to control *what capacity we allow these thoughts to transcend the present moment.*

APPLICATION

If digging into the past is too intense or painful (it can admittedly be a slippery slope), you can write down things like triggers, or negative or heavy emotions you are experiencing.

Take care of your heart this week. This exercise is only meant to help you confront these memories that haunt you. If you feel like you have a handle on them, and can place them where they belong (in the past) this might not serve you as it would someone who feels they cannot function because they are constantly being bombarded with these particular memories. You can use this application for many things, as mentioned above. This is ***your*** heart and soul work.

Take a sharpie and write the memories down on a ceramic tile. You can even draw pictures to represent them. Next, drop drops of rubbing alcohol over the tile and watch the ink spread and create a fantastic design (especially if you have colored colored permanent markers!).

You can use this tile as a coaster or mosaic it into a larger art piece. Every time you look at it in the future you can remember that you conquered this emotion. Yes - it will still hurt. Yes - the memories lying underneath are still things you won't want to dwell on, but this tile represents you taking control of your thoughts, your emotions and your future.

SELF-CARE

Give yourself permission to do something a little off the norm for you. Paint your toes a bold color, try some bohemian pants or flowing skirt on, buck the norm, explore a bit of wild and free in your life. It is liberating to feel free after being held captive by grief.

The vortex of grief demands your heart and soul from time to time. Grief is the cost of love, and one we pay so willingly. Be okay with wherever these moments take you. You will resurface. Stronger, better, braver.

....

....

....

....

....

....

....

....

....

....

....

....

....

....

....

....

....

....

....

FACETS OF GRIEF© ▼ *A creative approach to grief*

FACETS OF GRIEF© ▼ *A creative approach to grief*

letting it Out

ART THERAPY PROMPT 15

For the longest time I had a fantasy to take a stack of plates, smash them, and watch them as they would shatter against the pavement. I don't know why this image rolled in my head constantly, but it did. I imagine it has something to do with making my grief tangible, because so much of it was still such a mystery. And, as you can probably surmise - there was an intense brewing anger.

Fast forward about six years and I found out that there are actual places you can go and pay to smash dishes! I knew I must not be the only one. Whether people were smashing dishes to release anger, frustration or grief or all of the above, this is a very real thing.

Have you ever wanted to do something totally out of character after experiencing loss, that in another life you would consider violent or strange? Or maybe I should flip that question, who hasn't?

I communicated with another loss mom whom I met through her blog, in the early months of my grief through email. I still remember in one email she told me in all caps "YOU ARE NOT CRAZY!" I confessed that I wanted to punch something, break something and I felt so crazy. Her validation was everything I didn't even know I needed.

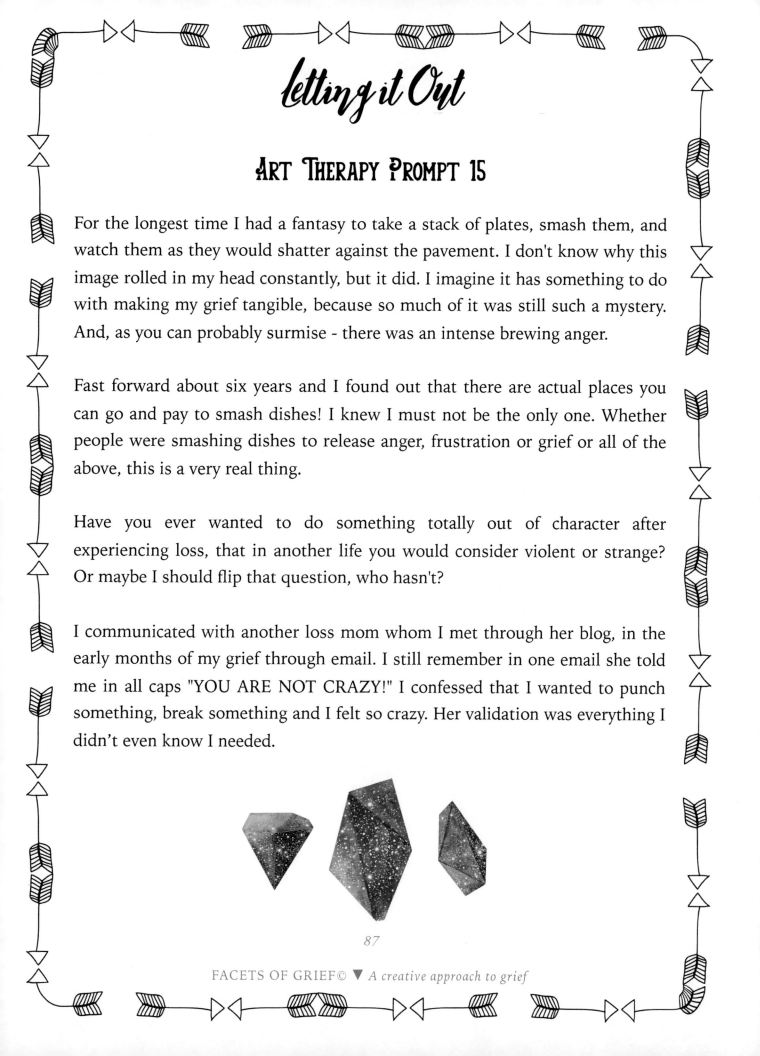

87

APPLICATION

Smash some plates. Grab some for cheap at a second hand or dollar store, or maybe you have some you'd be alright living without. Make it safe with no children or pets around. Protective eyewear. Closed-toe shoes. Spread a sheet or tarp down and smash away. You can even get a hammer or small tool involved to make the "smashing" more concise and constricted (think mosaic art). Be smart. Be safe.

If this isn't enticing or possible to you, you might try one of the following:

- shooting range
- taking some self-defense or kickboxing classes
- see if there is an actual plate smashing place in your area...
- find a punching bag and just go for it
- freeze water balloons and smash them (again safety here), release your feelings by breaking it apart with a hammer or chisel

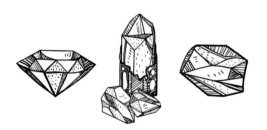

 SELF-CARE

Listen to a meditative podcast or YouTube channel. It might be someone calmly talking, it might be massage music, it might be natural sounds. Spend 5-10 minutes here.

It took one goodbye to wreck me, break me, make me, inspire me and shake me wildly
out of my comfort zone. There are some things you aren't meant to get over.

....

....

....

....

....

....

....

....

....

....

....

....

....

....

....

....

....

....

....

FACETS OF GRIEF© ▼ *A creative approach to grief*

··
··
··
··
··
··
··
··
··
··
··
··
··
··
··
··
··
··
··

FACETS OF GRIEF© ▼ *A creative approach to grief*

When Your Body Betrays You

Art Therapy Prompt 16

After the initial grief fog faded, I started becoming obsessed with medical clarification. In our own situation, the cause of death wasn't instantly clear or ever completely confirmed - we knew a lot of things were seriously wrong with our baby girl but we never had any tests come back positive. I went so far as to call the hospital and ask them to explain word for word what her cause of death was recorded as, since her death certificate was not enough information for me. I wanted to know what it meant, I wanted answers. I still remember the place I was when the woman on the other line had the awkward and difficult job of entertaining this grieving mother's wishes. But she did.

While I got medical explanations for what happened, it did nothing for my heart healing. In fact, it only made the questions even bigger. What was wrong with me? What kind of mother was I? How could my body turn on my own child this way? Could I trust this body to carry another child into the world? Could I trust it to do anything it was "supposed" to do? Was it something I breathed, ate, did or did not do?

The distrust I placed over my own body underscored everything about my life. How I ate, how I felt, how I dressed, how I interacted with others, how I felt about doing anything over the top and positive for myself. I felt unworthy and undeserving. It poured over into my relationships with everyone close to me. I felt disgusted because I felt hugely responsible for what happened.

Has grief torn the fabric of trust for your own body or self? How has it manifested itself in your life?

♡♡ APPLICATION

Do something ridiculously positive for just you this week. *Make sure it is at least one of these traits (the more the better):*

- healthy (mind, body or both)
- nourishing
- involves some kind of self-care
- guilt-free zone

Some ideas:

- Yoga
- Ride your bike
- Watch the sun set
- Knit, crochet, or try some handiwork
- Go watch a movie at the theatre - with a friend or without
- Aim to drink a gallon of water a day
- Diffuse essential oils at your desk, work station or car
- Get your nails done
- Get a massage
- Smile, and this time not for anyone else but you. This smile is a way to welcome peace into your life, and love.
- Purchase an adult coloring book and carve out some time to just color. If you want to go all in, try out Prisma colors. They blend together beautifully. Apparently coloring is a great alternative to meditation, according to psychologists.

♡ *Smiling is telling yourself you deserve to be happy again*

From that day on, there was a before and an after. Loss became the silent axis on which
her life would revolve.

....

....

....

....

....

....

....

....

....

....

....

....

....

....

....

....

....

....

FACETS OF GRIEF© ▼ *A creative approach to grief*

··

··

··

··

··

··

··

··

··

··

··

··

··

··

··

··

··

··

··

··

FACETS OF GRIEF© ▼ *A creative approach to grief*

Confronting the Inevitable

Art Therapy Prompt 17

A few months after we lost our baby, I accidentally stumbled into what many call the "baby loss community". For the first time since losing her, I didn't feel crazy and alone. I had wonderful real life friends and family who supported and loved me, but they also had no first hand experience in what I was feeling - even my loving and well-meaning husband.

In fact, nearly every night he saw me wrapped up in a blog, reading, and often crying. He would gently ask if I was alright, and eventually worked up the courage to ask me if all this reading/crying/looking at the sad pictures was a good idea. To any normal person, this looked like self-torture. But that couldn't be further than the truth. It was my release. It was my therapy, and eventually became more so when I started my own writing.

I never did have the chance to attend a real life support group, but I wonder sometimes where I might be if I had not found a community as loving and supportive as the one I found. I am still friends with many of the blogging bereaved mothers I "met" during this time.

A lot of the healing that transpired is largely due to this form of release and connection that happened those first few years, reading others' stories and writing through our own.

What is your release? Have you found one? You will know you have found your release when your takeaway is often nothing more than the opportunity to express your truest feelings. You will leave *fuller* in a sense - even if by a drop - than you were when you came. Expressing and releasing your emotions is vital to the healing process. It is giving your heart a chance to breathe, stretch, bend, shrink and expand again. It is our job to release them, allow them to take a physical or tangible form, and give your heart the freedom to discover what is left behind to pick up.

Broken pieces, but pieces of this precious life nonetheless.

♡♡ APPLICATION

List the emotions in your grief that take over most of your time and heart. Which ones weigh on you the most? Anger? Sadness? Depression? Loneliness? Emptiness? Rage? Jealousy? Indifference? Isolation? Fear? *Are there things, situations or even persons in your life that shut down your ability to express them?* Use this opportunity to release.

Take a giant piece of paper and draw a circle. Divide it into pie pieces and give larger pie pieces to the ones that take over more frequently. Reference the colors from your *Emotion Color Guide* if possible. The idea is the fling the paint onto the wheel. There might be nothing pretty or neat about this, but therapeutic? Absolutely. You could label each pie piece as well. Try to do this exercise once a month or every few months. You may see some transformation in the the size of the pie pieces. You can also do this on a small scale in your art journal.

Note: Playing some type of instrumental music (soundtracks are wonderful for this!) in the background will help get you focus on the exercise.

♥ SELF-CARE

Declutter a rom, a dresser drawer, a cabinet space or your computer desk.
"Have nothing in your house that you do not know to be useful or believe to be beautiful."
- William Morris

Love was at the beginning of all of this. Before loss, and before grief. It was love that opened her wounds and mended her scars daily. It was love that brought her to tears, and whispered the sweet memories back to her. And it would be love that would guide her home.

FACETS OF GRIEF© ▼ *A creative approach to grief*

Stitched Heart

Art Therapy Prompt 18

Strong is not a word I ever personally liked being described as, after our loss. But somehow that is usually how people tend to portray those of us who have been forced to live without one or more of our children. Strong. It is, of course, a wildly misleading illusion.

In the thick of grief, when I was accused of being strong, I felt like a fraud. In my mind, true strength is a voluntary act. It is some task you set out to do and give it your all. In this scenario, burying your own child does not qualify as strength, but rather a life sentence of the most intense pain you never signed up for.

BUT... now... more than seven years post loss, I can somewhat wrap my little head around the connection to strength that people associate with losing a child. It is a thought we ourselves would shudder to imagine, if we did not know this grief personally. It seems like only strong people can survive it. So it seems.

In reality, we are all made of flesh and bones, with the same blood pumping through our veins. We, grieving mothers, are no more capable of bearing this loss than the next person. We walk, we stand, we live, we breath the impossible and will until we breath our last breath.

Is is strength? I don't know, but it is telling of the resilience of the human spirit built inside of each of us to survive against all odds, and dare to love again in the impossible.

♡ APPLICATION

Use fabric scraps, any type of string, wire, permanent markers, thread and stuffing to create a stuffed, stitched up heart. *If you could hold your heart in your hand, what might it look like post grief?*

Is it vibrant again? Beating quickly? Struggling at best? Ready to embrace love again? Shattered? Torn? Refer to your Emotion Color Guide and decide what colors to incorporate. Would any words would be etched over your heart? What is holding it together? Soft threads of hope or harsh wires of the bitter valley of death?

1. Record your responses to the above in on paper any other ideas for your heart.
2. Cut out two fabric hearts. They can be the same, or different.
3. Take a needle and thread or your sewing machine and begin making stitches on over each side. The intention of this is to avoid neatness, unless of course that feels fitting for your heart visual. Messy and imperfection are welcome here! You can do this with different color threads and materials like wire and twine.
4. Use pens or permanent markers to write over it, if you wish. Embellish with buttons, ribbons, beads and anything else you can think of.
5. Repeat this process for the back side.
6. When both sides resonate with you, you can begin the process of stitching both sides (pattern/ color side facing out) together. Leave a small hole to push the stuffing in, and then finish up the stitch with a double knot. *Embrace the messiness.* Grief is messy.

 SELF-CARE

Spend the first five minutes of your day in silence. This can be a perfect time for devotions, quiet time, meditation, prayer, easy stretching, deep breathing, or yoga. The goal is mindfulness and to start your day with intention, instead of letting the day rule you.

I am not there yet, but I am closer than I was yesterday.

....

....

....

....

....

....

....

....

....

....

....

....

....

....

....

....

FACETS OF GRIEF© ▼ *A creative approach to grief*

Creating New Dreams

ART THERAPY PROMPT 19

It becomes a science. Dodging the inevitable triggers. The places, the smells, the faces that remind of us of the other life we feel and believe we were meant to live. An alternate universe. A parallel one, but so very different. In fact it couldn't be more different.

The science we have mastered to inhale deeply (just in the knick of time), push in a positive thought or prayer before completely losing it in front of the realtor, banker, cashier or teacher. Cracking the smile, laughing even (feignedly, but who can tell, really?) at frivolity. It is all frivolity after death of a child. Madness even. We really are not applauded nearly enough for our skills to hone our emotions. We feel like a basket case, but in almost no time at all, we are the ones who should be walking down the red carpet for Academy Award nominations.

We act. We pretend. And to our own detriment, we convince. And so naturally, the world spins rapidly around us, expecting us to catch up, move on, get on with life. We are left disheveled, not ready to join in on the madness but often unable to communicate the gap between how we appear to feel and how we really feel. We do ourselves so much disservice with all the pretense.

Are you amazed at your ability to hide your grief and pain? Or at the very least bewildered? I can say that I have felt this about myself, but not in the boastful way it might imply. This ability to hide the most intense and raw pain has left me confused, conflicted and often guilty. While there are times I have believed it was most beneficial, even for me, to conceal my truest feelings, there were certainly times I feel it could have resulted in healing in letting it out in some way or form.

♡♡ APPLICATION

Think of the dream catcher for a few moments. It is a Native American tradition which was believed to filter bad dreams and only allow good dreams through. The center is a net to catch. The feathers or streamers that flow downward are meant to release and drip only the good. While I am not Native American, and don't believe that any one object can do this, I do believe there is power in releasing and expressing. Use this idea of the dreamcatcher to work through your grief. Think of the dreamcatcher's center as the net to capture all the negative. The triggers. The intense pain. The hardest feelings and emotions to draw out and deal with. Think of the spacing in which the feathers flow down and all around the dreamcatcher as the good. What should you be filtering through, and allowing to take up your heart and mind? What things can you mindfully rest your soul in?

You can simply draw a dream catcher or use the template on the next page. To draw simply draw a circle in your journal or a piece of paper, and for the feathers, you can draw a few elongated ovals or wavy, flowing lines downward. After filling the center with the negative, you can tape pieces thread or yarn over the center to create the dream catcher's net. Think about the things that filter through the dream catcher's net, and then write them all around your dream catcher. Alternatively, if you're feeling crafty and adventurous, you can make a dream catcher, and meditate on these ideas as you create one and use your art journal to write about them.

♡ SELF-CARE

Take a little time to think about your abilities and talents. Your gifts to this world. Write down three things you are good at or have been in the past. It can be things you are known for (your apple pie recipe, your voice, green thumb, ability to make people laugh, your mastered messy-hair-bun-that-always-gets-compliments, etc), things you are proud of yourself for learning, things that make you feel more like yourself.

Creating and Releasing Dreams

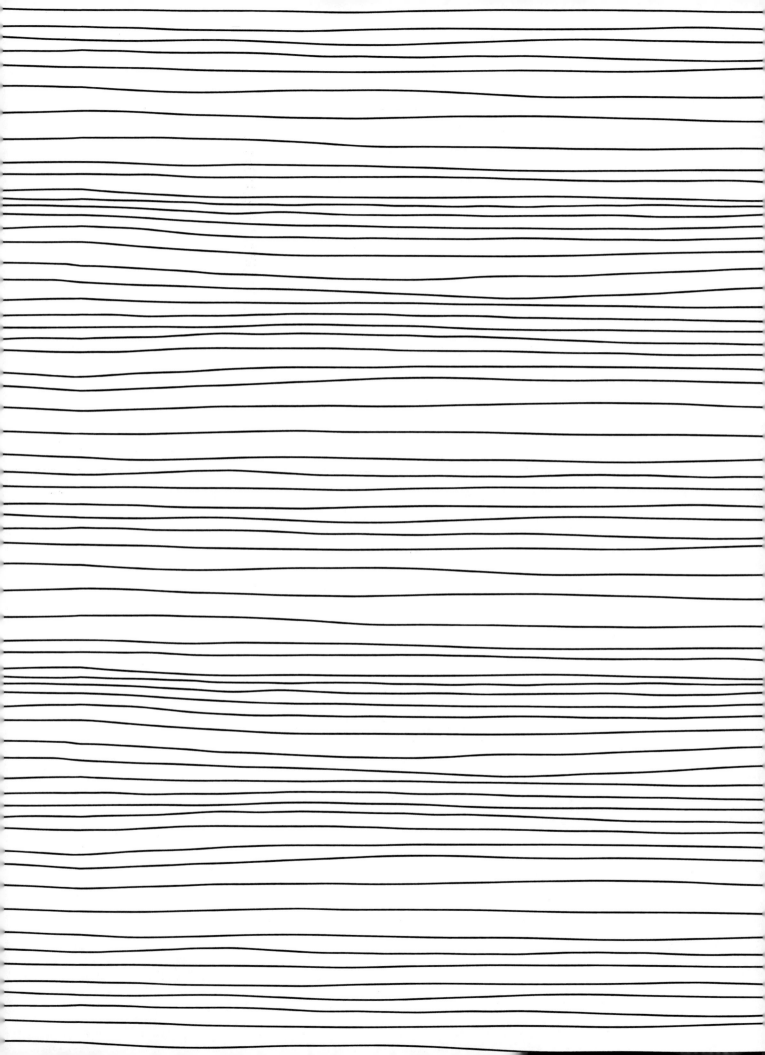

A mother is not defined by the number of children you can see,
but by the love she holds in her heart.

··

··

··

··

··

··

··

··

··

··

··

··

··

··

··

··

··

The Fear of Forgetting

Art Therapy Prompt 20

The resistance to find happiness again after loss was met by many obstacles but one of the earliest ones was the fear of forgetting. Forgetting her smell, the way she wrapped her entire hand around my index finger, seeing her eyes open and explore the world for the first time and so many more "little" things. I never wanted to forget. So I clung to the memories and held onto them like my life depended on them (it did), and little did I know that in time the memories would never fade, but the intense sadness could and would be replaced with this unspeakable joy and thankfulness that she was ever mine.

I don't know when or how it all happened, but I somehow started releasing this sadness that held me captive. I think it all boiled down to not wanting her entire existence to be responsible for my ultimate ruining. She was amazing. I wanted my life to reflect every bit of the light she brought into our lives. It was not an overnight experience, but little by little I found the courage to allow the memories and sadness to unravel and settle into two separate corners of my heart. Co-existing but no longer dependent on one another, if that makes any sense at all. Sadness will always underline these memories, but only because I know that's all we'll ever have. Those memories in and of themselves are pure joy. Are you afraid of forgetting precious memories? Are you able to think on them without sadness overwhelming you?

111

APPLICATION

Make a paper bead necklace. Draw tall, elongated triangles about 2-3 inches tall onto a colored or patterned sheet of paper. Cut about 8 of these. Write your memories down on these triangles. Alternatively, you can take a sheet of paper and finish the sentences below on the triangles:

I never...
I wonder...
I wish...

Wrap into beads and secure with tape of pretty stickers, Mod Podge or a glue gun. Keep a small opening in the very center to string the beads onto a string or twine. You can even make earrings or bracelets out of these. Think about what you'd like to wear. Wearing your most precious memories with your baby seems like a pretty awesome way to keep them close!

SELF-CARE

Visit a book store and travel into a section that is calling you (nothing on grief or loss or anything sad allowed for this one!). Travel. Languages. Non-fiction. Biographies of fascinating people. Fiction. Something completely distracting to dive into. History. A hobby section like gardening, crafting, arts...

She didn't remain in the darkness because she couldn't get over her loss, but because she didn't know how to exist in the light anymore. Everything about the light felt unnatural and like a complete betrayal to the universe she lost.

....

....

....

....

....

....

....

....

....

....

....

....

....

....

....

....

....

....

....

FACETS OF GRIEF© ▼ *A creative approach to grief*

··
··
··
··
··
··
··
··
··
··
··
··
··
··
··
··
··
··
··

FACETS OF GRIEF© ▼ *A creative approach to grief*

Grief is...

Art Therapy Prompt 21

If you could describe grief as one tangible thing, what would it be? Throughout the years this questions has had a variety of answers. In the beginning I might have likened it to a tsunami. The word catastrophe was so fitting for how my life felt. Damaged and catastrophic.

When the numbness wore off and reality started to set in, it was like hugging a cactus. Something that needed to be done, but the pain was searing. As the years went on, a cave or an abyss felt spot on because grief is so desperately lonely. Today I think about it as an exotic flower. Mysterious, wild, untamable, a sweet fragrance, but only because I can fully wrap my mind around the conclusion that this strange emotion of grief only exists where love lived first.

APPLICATION

Of course, all my examples are elements from nature and you can certainly find a plethora of examples in our natural environments to "personify" grief, but if you feel led in another direction don't let my illustrations box you in. Feel free to explore.

If you could illustrate grief as something tangible, or describe it as something, what would it be and why? Often these images are crystal clear in our subconscious. My examples aren't things I thought deeply about. I felt like I could reach out and physically touch the prickly bristles of a cactus when my world was drowning in a sea of triggers and reminders. What picture comes to mind when grief is heavy on your heart? Why do you feel these images surface? Have these images taken on new forms throughout time? You can write about this prompt in your journal or cut and paste clip art of your images into your art journal, or do a little of both.

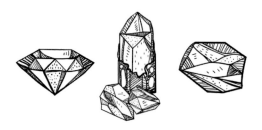

♡SELF-CARE

Get a hold of some bath bombs this week and unwind in a warm bath. You can also make your own bath bombs with this simple recipe!

She wept. Because life was so full. Of hurts. Of joys.
Of the madness that danced between the two.

···

···

···

···

···

···

···

···

···

···

···

···

···

···

···

···

···

···

FACETS OF GRIEF© ▼ *A creative approach to grief*

FACETS OF GRIEF© ▼ *A creative approach to grief*

Keeping Their Memory Alive

Art Therapy Prompt 22

On Daughter's Day one year, I had the revisitation of that strange ache that comes out of left field, that can only be explained by the never-ending love of a mother heart. Even though we have been blessed with another daughter since our loss, that ache for *her* still pulses under the surface and I suppose it always will. Any celebration also bears a silent ache, and I wouldn't have it any other way. **Grief is love...** I remind myself on the hard days.

In the very beginning of my grief I would take every opportunity I had to talk about Jenna. The awkward glances and shuffling ensued over the course of the first few months, and I eventually began to understand. Death is an unnecessary crunch on everyday conversation. An inconvenient topic and most of all, uncomfortable. I responded with holding back. I started keeping her inside. I shrunk back from baby and "mommy" conversations, because I understood the few memories I had in the NICU with Jenna really put a damper on parallel stories with children still living. I needed to share her life, but I also hated people unconsciously associating my daughter with nothing more than a tragedy. She was still my baby, and I was still a mother.

As months developed into years, I continued to keep her to myself, but not because I was afraid of the way it would be received, but because some people just weren't worthy. They would not be able to grasp just she could still be such a gift, even in death, so I became picky who I shared her with. When I discovered Pregnancy and Infant Loss Awareness Day, I relished in the opportunity to celebrate, remember and share her with others. It wasn't imposing on baby conversations, instead it was an intentional way to shed light on children who are desperately missed. A time just for them.

♡♡ APPLICATION

Is there a day or event that you celebrate your child's life? October 15th is just one example that has walks all over the world. Google "Pregnancy and Infant Loss Walk" and your city/town/country and there might be something in your area. A lot of people who haven't been successful in finding an existing walk start one of their own. In October I like to purchase a new beautiful candle for Jenna. You can buy one, or even customize one this year using the tutorial below. You will want to create the image(s) you want and make them the size of your candle on your computer using a photo editing software. You can even use your child's footprints, hand prints or ultrasound pictures in this project if you have them available to you.

Customized Candle Tutorial
Supplies: candle, tissue paper, heat tool or hair dryer, wax paper

1. Secure a piece of tissue paper firmly to a sheet of printing paper using a glue stick, or taping all edges. Once you have found the image you want and you have edited it to the size you need to fit your candle you print it off on tissue paper. Trim your image leaving as little border as possible and the place it *ink side out* on your candle.

2. Wrap a piece of wax paper tightly around your candle, holding both ends in one hand on the back side (you might want to wear an oven mitt for this part!) For the next step you can use an embossing gun, hairdryer or even your stove. Holding your candle with your hands away from the heat slowly heat until you see the wax paper start to melt and you see the ink come through the paper . At that point, you're done. Carefully peel the wax paper away and reveal your printed candle.

♡ SELF-CARE

Write a love note to yourself on a sticky note and place it somewhere where you can read it each morning or evening. You are brave. You are a beautiful mother. You have a mother heart. You are worth it all.

Grief is so overwhelming you don't grasp how much has changed until time has allowed you to adapt to the massive ripples that have saturated the topography of your entire life. Time doesn't heal - it merely gives you a measurable space to adapt to this new normal.

···

···

···

···

···

···

···

···

···

···

···

···

···

···

···

···

···

···

···

···

FACETS OF GRIEF© ▼ *A creative approach to grief*

The Lies From Grief

Art Therapy Prompt 23

It is usually the quietest voice that has the most credibility, and conversely the least amount of attacks. Grief can be fierce, and loud and accusing. In my own experience it has accused me of not being enough, not doing enough, not being strong enough, or vulnerable enough. Not being happy enough and even sad enough. When I got victory over the accusations coming toward me personally, these thoughts turned on the people who were earnestly trying to help, in spite of their clumsy efforts. They often failed because that is what humans do well, when they don't know what to do. Buried deep in my grief hole, my outlook on life was narrow and dark, and their failures was all I could see for the longest time. Their failure to understand, their failure to give me space and room and freedom to do this my way. I could not see past my own hurt and that their intentions were honorable. I felt rushed, judged and misunderstood.

When you are grieving your world is completely and rightfully all about *you*. It is about your child too, but mostly you. You are the one breathing and fighting to survive this impossible new life that hardly feels like living at all. You are the one trying to keep your head above the water and learning to swim again. Grief has a way of making our world all about our pain, and we can become quickly convinced that the "non-bereaved" will never say/do/think/act the right way. It is easy to write them all off entirely, and for me personally I reached a point that I kept everyone who had not suffered a child loss at arm's length. I was tired of being hurt. This was pain I felt I could have some control over. I did not have to be continually hurt by others too. I didn't have a say in the pain over my dead daughter, but this I did. Grief had me convinced that I would never be able to connect with an outside world and I was convinced I wouldn't ever want to again.

♡♡ APPLICATION

Put grief on trial. Interrogate grief. Challenge your heart to put this emotion that has worn you to a crisp on trial, and ask her some hard questions. She has been your friend and foe, and possibly your only tangible connection to your child. It might feel like betrayal to treat her like an enemy.

What is she telling you that keeps you in a dark place?
What evidence does she have? Solid facts? Is it circumstantial evidence? Or assumptions?
Is it possible that grief might be isolating you, exaggerating the truth?
Are the things she is telling you lifting you up? Or are they dragging you down? How is this place she is pulling you toward serving your in your healing?

Grief is our love language, it is the only way to mother our dead children, but we can challenge our grief and some of her lies. We can challenge her to wash up some buried treasures. Some truths. Some facts. Some refreshing perspectives. Maybe someone has hurt you. Maybe you did not feel included at a function. Or maybe you felt like someone did not want to engage in a conversation with you about your child who has passed. Grief might be correct. But then again, she could be exaggerating and exploiting your pain. And in the case that she is telling the truth, and it hurts your heart challenge yourself to silence that voice. How does it help to fuel this pain daily or constantly? Challenge yourself to take control of the thoughts grief stirs up. Write down the thoughts you are ready to challenge and let go of. Tear them up, burn them or blot them out with paint in your art journal. You could even save the torn/ burned pieces and collage them into your journal.

♥ SELF-CARE

Plan an evening to stargaze. Drive away from the city lights and noise. Follow the moon and stop when the stars get bigger and brighter. Bring some tunes, a warm blanket and consider asking someone to come with you.

I once thought I had love figured out. And then I met grief.

· ·

· ·

· ·

· ·

· ·

· ·

· ·

· ·

· ·

· ·

· ·

· ·

· ·

· ·

· ·

· ·

· ·

· ·

FACETS OF GRIEF© ▼ *A creative approach to grief*

FACETS OF GRIEF© ▼ *A creative approach to grief*

Everything is Different

ART THERAPY PROMPT 24

Before experiencing grief I thought I had it all figured out. Who I was. What I wanted. What I believed. What was next to check off my life list.

For me that looked like finishing school, and then getting pregnant. Life was going peachy -- until it wasn't. After returning to our sad and empty two bedroom rental home, I was faced with the grim reality that so many parents before me had come to know all too well. Life is fragile, and terribly unpredictable. Things that happen to "other people" can happen to you too. Nothing tasted the same, felt the same or looked the same. My own reflection in the mirror, sunlight, church, conversations, grocery trips, driving, it all felt so different, and so pointless. From a very young age, I had this burning desire to see exotic places, and travel the world and feed the poor and visit mission fields, and for the first time in my life the only place I longed to visit was Heaven. My dreams weren't even the same.

It goes without saying that grief will change things in your life, and in some cases - absolutely everything. It penetrates into every area of our lives, and in ways we don't ever anticipate. Especially at first. That is probably the one thing about grief that blew me away early on. The power, the endless reach, the finality of it's existence and the permanent way it divides my life into a *before* and an *after*. I swing the door wide open to grief when my daughter died, because it was the only physical, emotional and spiritual way I could mother her.

♡♡ APPLICATION

What about you? What things in your life have changed the most? It could surprisingly be for the **better** or for the **worse**.

Make a list. Big things. Little things. Things that maybe only you notice.

What things bother you? What things are you okay with? Does anything surprise you about your lists?

Try flipping through an old magazine and clip out pictures that resonate with your lists and create a page (or a few) to illustrate this point. You could even do a "before and after" scenario. What things were like, and how they have changed. You can use cut out words and text too.

♡ SELF-CARE

On a sunny day lay on the grass and watch the clouds roll by. Relax, and let your mind go. Be intentional about keeping your mind on this moment, that might mean keeping your phone on silent or away from you during this exercise.

Because when you lose your child, without knowing it, you expect your world to cater to your grief. You naively believe the world will stop spinning on it's axis, so that daylight never shines on this desolate land you've inherited. Light feels like betrayal to this barren wasteland.

FACETS OF GRIEF© ▼ *A creative approach to grief*

132

fear

ART THERAPY PROMPT 25

If there is anything that has lingered in grief in this life post loss for me personally, it would hands down be fear. I have drowned in sadness, threw paint and words around when anger was more than I could bear, but fear had the farthest reach, the deepest impact and a sly way of wrecking my peace and healing for the long haul.

Fear is sneaky. It transcends into your soul. It makes you keenly aware of how fragile, unpredictable, unfair and cruel life can be. It confronts you with your own mortality, your child's mortality, your spouse, and each of your loved ones' mortality. You become a little obsessed with what if scenarios, and nightmares are not uncommon. You are convinced that your fear is a necessary precaution, when in fact it is just fear on steroids. Your sleep and day to day routine suffers as a result. Fear takes a horrible tragedy that you have watched in a movie or read about in a news story and makes it your own. You are the people you have watched and read about. These horrible, unspeakable things happened to you. You are not immune, and fear capitalizes on everything death has just pushed into your world. How has fear manifested in your life after loss? Has fear played a role in your grief, loss and/ or healing? To what degree?

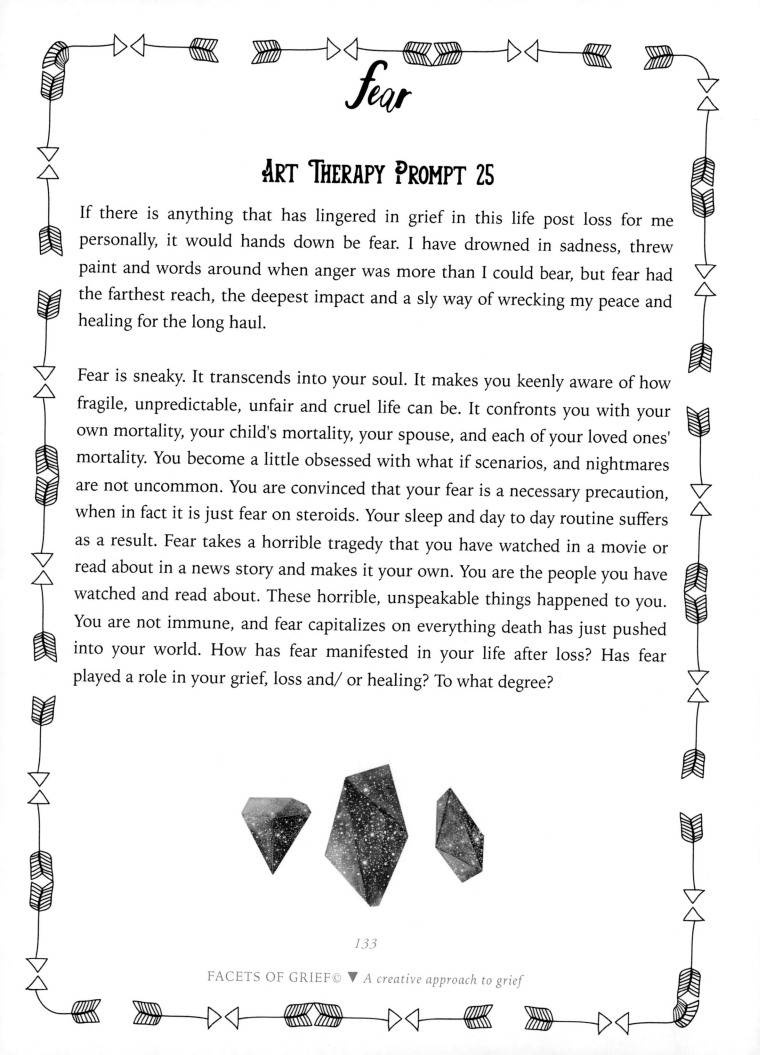

133

♡♡ APPLICATION

Four Square Feelings

Supplies: strips of paper (different colors for different emotions is optional), writing tools, magazines, scissor, glue or glue sticks

1. Write the emotion you want to tackle on a strip of paper.
2. Take a sheet of paper (the same color as the one you used for #1 if you're using various colors to represent different emotions)
3. Fold your paper into four squares.
4. In the first quadrant write down 3-5 synonyms for your emotion.
5. In the second quadrant cut out pictures or words that represent fear or your emotion.
6. In the third quadrant write down scenarios that stir up this emotion or trigger it.
7. In the last quadrant Google names of books, essays, movies and TV shows that have this emotion in the title (can also include synonyms).

You can also draw this out in your art journal instead of using a separate sheet of paper, or paste it in.

♡ SELF-CARE

Stop to smell some roses, and pick some. Pick yourself a bouquet. Or maybe in your part of the world fall means oranges, reds and yellows (in which case I'm a tad jealous! ;). Collect a bouquet of leaves!! Keep your loot in your art journal.

No one ever told me that grief felt so like fear. - C.S. LEWIS

....
....
....
....
....
....
....
....
....
....
....
....
....
....
....
....
....
....

FACETS OF GRIEF© ▼ *A creative approach to grief*

···
···
···
···
···
···
···
···
···
···
···
···
···
···
···
···
···
···
···
···

FACETS OF GRIEF© ▼ *A creative approach to grief*

Words and Affirmations

Art Therapy Prompt 26

Many have survived this before you.
Many will endure this pain after you.
You will survive this.
And you are capable of so much more than surviving this.

Have you reckoned with this truth?
Do you believe it?
Does it feel attainable? Impossible? Like someone else's story?

It can be your truth too. The reality of this will totally and completely depend on you. Not anyone else, and certainly not time.

It matters what you fill your time with, what company you decide to share - in person and in words, how often and deeply you allow yourself to sink into sadness, anger, loneliness, jealousy, depression or anything else taking over your heart. Grief is anything but a party. None of it is easy, but ironically it is easy to get stuck in one space of grief. Whether it is sadness, or anger or anything else.

Have you felt "stuck" in a space in grief? I refuse to call them stages, because it suggests that you should be traveling through them in a particular order - which of course is totally ridiculous. Matters of the heart cannot be boxed in or wrapped up into pretty little bows. Grief doesn't come with a map, only with a heart full of love with no place to call home.

♡♡ APPLICATION

There is power in mantras. What words pick you up on a particularly awful day? Is it scripture? A quote? A song? An unspoken word, like a kind gesture or smile?

Consider writing your mantra onto a rock, as a vision rock. Keep it with you wherever you go, or place it somewhere you will see it often or where triggers happen frequently. The bigger the rock, the longer the quote can be. You can use sharpie markers, paint, chalk paint markers, magazine text clip outs just to name a few ideas.

 SELF-CARE

Consider making a few more vision rocks. You could even do this on bigger smooth sticks and branches. Paint symbols that remind you of your child or patterns. Write more mantras and affirmations. Get messy. Make this an outdoor activity if weather permits.

Be exceptional. Be broken. Be ready to heal. Be whatever it is you need to be, but above all else be brave enough to break the rules on grief. Again and again and again.

140

··

··

··

··

··

··

··

··

··

··

··

··

··

··

··

··

··

··

Full or Empty

ART THERAPY PROMPT 27

It's almost like you need to recalibrate your needs and personal settings. To verbalize what made me feel "*full*" after Jenna died would have been confusing to say the least. Nothing made me feel "full". Not anyone's company, words, food, gifts or visits. They all meant something, but none of them could ever give me back the only thing I wanted. I was left feeling empty all of the time. But there were things that made grief worse, and drained me even more than normal life. So my recalibration started with recognizing what made my grief worse, and in time I actually did find circumstances or things that made me feel an elevation in spirit, or "full", or was overall *less draining*...

Things like engaging in normal conversation, going out, faking a smile at a social function, in the early days of grief left me feeling depleted emotionally. A couple of years into grief, I did narrow down things that helped me feel full. For me, they were time alone to write, hot tea, yoga, live music, dancing and instrumental music on YouTube.

And as my grief grew, I found a longer, more defining list of things that either completely emptied me or poked small holes and left me draining slowly. Most of these involved certain complex relationships, faith issues and trouble trusting myself again (in pregnancy, parenting and so forth).

♡♡ APPLICATION

Create a Full or Empty diagram in your art journal.

1. Put your name in the center of the circle, in the middle of the page.
2. Using a colored pen, write at the end of the arrows going "out" of your center circle the activities, experiences, circumstances of feelings that deplete you.
3. Using a different colored pen, write on arrows sign "in" what nurtures, energizes, enriches or just feels good to you.
4. Count the number of arrows in and the arrows out.
5. What does this tell you about your life? Is there something off balance? Do some adjustments need to be made? Use this visual to help you decide what can stay and what needs to be go.

♥ SELF-CARE

As women, we are prone to multitask, even when the circumstances don't require our Olympic efforts to do it all. We carry so much responsibility on our shoulders, whether we stay at home, work, single, married or anything else. Slow down, and do just one thing at a time. No multitasking for an hour, or a day or a week. Whatever your life can afford. Be intentional, slow, and think about how your toes feel, how your jaw feels, how your shoulder blades feel. Is there tension? You might need to take it slower, and breathe. Let the tension fall away. If there was tension anywhere in your body, take this exercise with you throughout your day, to let release unnecessary tension.

It went something like this:
Once upon a time... The end.
And yet here I am. Living an impossible story with an ending I never expected.

....

....

....

....

....

....

....

....

....

....

....

....

....

....

....

....

....

....

FACETS OF GRIEF© ▼ *A creative approach to grief*

When Gratitude Feels Impossible

Art Therapy Prompt 28

I cannot count how many times I have been told to be thankful. Be thankful you are still young, still healthy, still have this, still have that, still able to this or that, and on it goes.

Fill in the blanks. When life sucker punches us, kicks us, knocks us over, turns our world inside out and through the ring of fire, we often feel we are being shamed out of our pain and dragged into this blinding light to JUST. BE. THANKFUL.

The worst and best part is that all this is being done with the best of intentions. It's no secret that a thankful heart is nearly the opposite of one that is drowning in pity and pain.

These people, they are on to something... but are naively going about this the wrong way.

In my own world, I felt deeper pain when I was told to be thankful. First of all, I knew what I had, and now on top of the original pain, I felt guilt for not showing enough gratitude for what was already mine.

I wrote years ago, a blog post, and at the end there is a line that haunted me the moment I typed it. It was one of those posts I wrote through ugly tears one late night at the peak of holiday season. I knew it was true, and I knew I was riding the fence between these two worlds. Seeing it in word form was a wake up call, and a little startling because I wasn't sure where I'd land in the end.

"You know that you can die bitter, or die thankful. There is no in between."

While you might feel completely incapable of writing anything down in your list of things to be thankful for, I challenge you to open your heart to a different perspective on finding gratefulness, even in brokenness. Gratitude isn't Thanksgiving or turkeys or thinking of and naming off all the things you should be thankful for.

As incredulous as it may seem, beautiful things, the things we should be thankful for hurt too. They hurt because our whole world hurts. Every fragment of happiness and life feels like a violation to our brokenness.

How dare the sun shine!
How can the birds be singing after what happened?
How dare I laugh at something hysterical after what happened!

Needless to say thankful is not our forte in brokenness. Brokenness isn't exactly the breeding ground for overflowing gratitude, *unless* you step outside the box for a moment.

I like to challenge us grieving mothers to see gratitude as counting the things that aren't making our frame of mind, our day, our lives, our pain *worse*. Because, let's be honest — nothing can make it better. Nothing. So asking a broken person to be thankful for what they have is pointless. They see what they have, and frankly, it isn't enough (whether the person giving this advice agrees or not).

So let's start there. What isn't making your pain worse? Whose company doesn't leave you wanting to smash plates or tear up a punching bag? What movie doesn't intensity your pain and even helps you forget your pain for a few minutes?

APPLICATION

Start with little expectation. For starters, let's talk about *what gratitude will not do*:

- make your pain go away
- make things better
- make you forget what happened
- cure you
- heal you
- erase what happened
- help you move on

Instead, practicing gratitude will:

- help you be intentional about where you let your mind wander, and dwell
- help you recognize things that are helping you, and not helping you grieve/ heal/ be
- help you take control of your life

Notice how all these things that it *will do*, affect one person - you. Of course, there are many things that could be added to both lists, but that mostly depends on, again – *you*. You are the pilot in control of your destination. Gratitude after experiencing loss isn't impossible, but it also doesn't look like the traditional image of giving thanks. At the core of gratitude is control, and that is what I love about *choosing* gratitude. Being grateful is choosing to be mindful, choosing control, choosing happiness or peace on some level, choosing yourself again. In your art journal or below on the journaling pages, jot down some things that fit this definition/ idea of gratitude. What things/ people/ circumstances aren't making your life harder or worse?

 SELF-CARE

Create peaceful rituals. It can be drinking lemon water every morning, or meeting your day
with your bare feet and morning dew. Create simple easy to do rituals that ground your day
and you'll find your way "home" no matter what life throws at you.

The only things certain in her life anymore were her broken heart and empty arms that kept her awake at night. Everything else felt like someone else's reality. But the pain was too keen and her love was too great to be someone else's story.

....

....

....

....

....

....

....

....

....

....

....

....

....

....

....

....

....

....

....

FACETS OF GRIEF© ▼ *A creative approach to grief*

··
··
··
··
··
··
··
··
··
··
··
··
··
··
··
··
··
··
··

FACETS OF GRIEF© ▼ *A creative approach to grief*

Visualization

Art Therapy Prompt 29

There is something about tragic world events that strokes our own personal loss in a unique and painful way. Maybe it is because our hearts have expanded with an enormous capacity for empathy towards tragedies, unthinkable disasters and things that only happen to *"other"* people.

How have the recent current events in the world resonated with you? Not politically, but personally. Has it affected your grief at all? Your healing? Your thought pattern? Your empathy towards those affected? Has it surprised you how much or how little the recent unfolding of events affected you?

APPLICATION

Create a concrete poem. Concrete poetry—sometimes also called 'shape poetry'—is poetry whose visual appearance matches the topic of the poem. The words form shapes which illustrate the poem's subject as a picture, as well as through their literal meaning. This type of poetry has been used for thousands of years, since the ancient Greeks began to enhance the meanings of their poetry by arranging their characters in visually pleasing ways back in the 3rd and 2nd Centuries BC.

Firstly, choose a shape for your poem. Some ideas are symbols that make you think of your child, favorite animals, shapes, etc.

1. Draw a simple outline of a shape or trace an image in your art journal with pencil.
2. Write a draft of your poem on a regular sheet of paper. Describe how the subject makes you feel, why you chose it, etc. The words will be fitted into your drawing, so make it as long as you like. ***Good news - it doesn't have to rhyme!***
3. Lightly in pencil, write your poem into the shape. It's ok if it doesn't fit properly yet, because this is where you find out if you need to make the writing larger or smaller, maybe even play with various size text and doodling.
4. Decide if you need to make your writing bigger or smaller in certain parts of the drawing, then erase your first draft and write out the poem again. You can keep doing this until you feel a finished piece has been created.
5. Finally, erase the outline of your shape, so that it is just the words from your poem left creating the image. If you were writing in pencil, you can now go over the words in pen or a permanent marker.

If you're lost on the drawing aspect of this exercise, you print out a shape from the web of an image you'd like to use for your concrete poem and fill in the words.

SELF-CARE

Add some color to your plate. Add some berries, pineapple, collard greens, sliced applies, sweet potatoes or whatever is in season in your part of the world. The more colors the better.

Post loss is also post innocence. There is no escaping the knowing. And that might be the crux of this whole living and embracing life again. Knowing it could all happen again.

....

....

....

....

....

....

....

....

....

....

....

....

....

....

....

....

....

....

FACETS OF GRIEF© ▼ *A creative approach to grief*

··

··

··

··

··

··

··

··

··

··

··

··

··

··

··

··

··

··

··

FACETS OF GRIEF© ▼ *A creative approach to grief*

Holidays

ART THERAPY PROMPT 30

It's okay if you're feeling anxious, distant and/ or dreading the holidays. It's equally okay if you're embracing them on some level too. You're biggest task is before you as plates of food are being passed around topped with light conversations and no doubt interactions with people you don't talk to frequently, thanks to family gatherings. This often means you are re-telling a lot of your story, or even worse trying your best to keep it together when you really want to fall apart. Be gentle on yourself, and breathe. Escape as often as you need to. God knows I spent a lot of time composing myself in peoples' bathrooms. Social gathering is exhausting, and it's no wonder really. We are pressured into feeling okay, into conversations we can't possibly care about, and forced to learn about other peoples' happy outcomes, pregnancies, announcements and on it goes.

You don't need to be a grouch or obnoxious on purpose, but realize the work you are doing this very minute and for the rest of your life is incredible. Give yourself some grace. Don't be afraid to speak up about how you're feeling. I hope that you are surrounded by at least one person that can be flexible around the time and space your heart might need, but my biggest hope for you during the holidays is that they aren't as awful as you may anticipate. Anticipation is usually the worst part of any scenario.

♡♡ APPLICATION

With lots of food being passed around these next few weeks, making a remembrance plate is a small way to include your child in the holidays. Some of these might not be food safe, but they could still be used for decoration, gifts, and even applied to other things aside from plates. These all involve cheap white ceramic plates you can pick up at the dollar store, permanent markers and some involve special paints. Maybe one of these ideas will resonate with you. There are a few ways to go about this. My favorite is using hand prints and/or footprints. If you have a stamp of your child's prints you can easily do this. (You can make a rubber stamp from them if you have a photocopy of them. Usually your local printer can guide you on how to achieve this. There are dozens of online stamp companies that can do this for you as well.

You will want to make sure to invest in a permanent stamp pad ink if you have a stamp to use.

For the lettering use a permanent marker. This can be done on a dollar store plate. After creating you design on a ceramic dish, let it air dry for 24 hours and then bake at 350* for 20 minutes. Another thing you can try is making abstract lines, or writing a poem on a plate with the sharpies. It can be a poem that makes you think of your child, lyrics, or a verse. You can incorporate colors and themes from your Emotion Color Guide as well.

♡ SELF-CARE

Step outside and collect some pine cones, or dry leaves, twigs, rocks, stones, whatever might be in your surroundings. You might have access to roses. Dried roses are just as beautiful as fresh ones. Create a nature mandala with your findings. You could bring them inside if it's too cold to do this outside. Let this mandala be the release of any anxiety or fear you might have during the holidays. Embrace this as an opportunity to generate courage within yourself. You might not feel the joy, or the merriness of it all, but you will survive.

You won't surface without scars. You won't learn to breathe again without practically suffocating. And you won't be able to ever say that could never happen to me - because it did. But you will rise, and you will find. You will come through this.

··
··
··
··
··
··
··
··
··
··
··
··
··
··
··
··
··
··
··
··
··

FACETS OF GRIEF© ▼ *A creative approach to grief*

Remind Yourself

Art Therapy Prompt 31

It is so easy to forget the good things that you are. Yes, you. We are champions at beating ourselves up. It is so easy to let yourself fall down that rabbit hole of the what-ifs, giving yourself literal headaches over what you could have done better, differently, etc. The list of things that have the capacity to make our world worse is endless. This is your challenge to give yourself a breather. A mindful way to practice self-care. A deliberate love toward you. An appreciation for what you bring to this world.

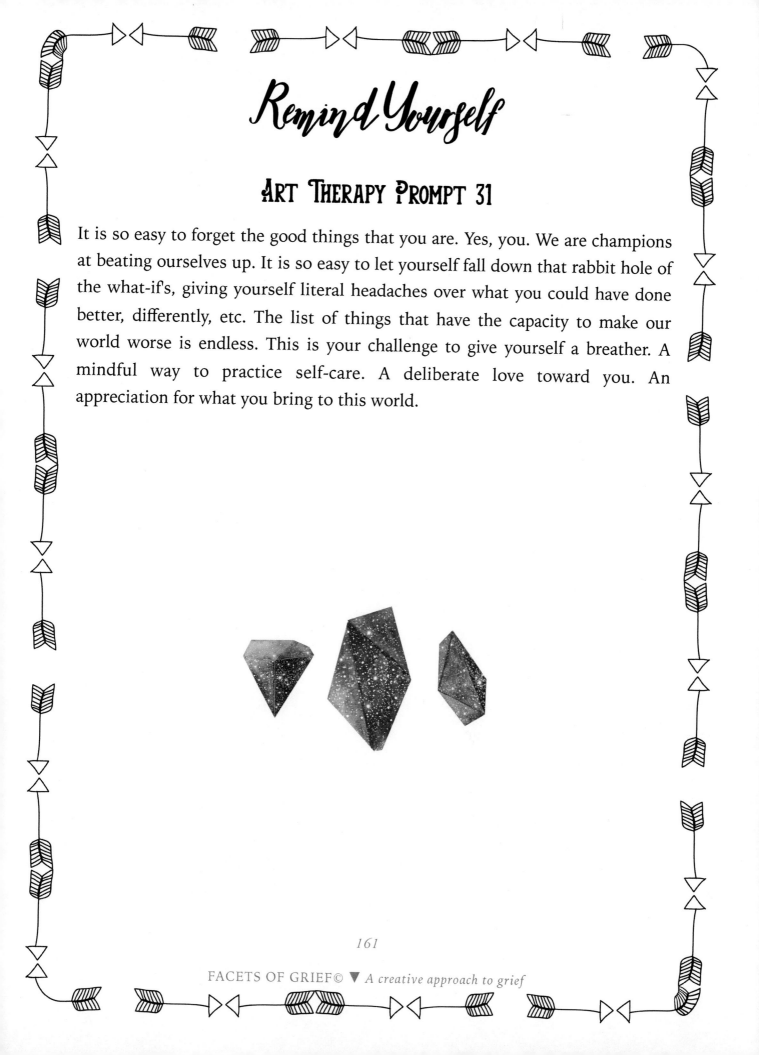

♡♡ APPLICATION

Create a "Take One" flyer for your grief. Take a few moments in a place alone, with music and maybe candles and few electronic distractions. Allow your mind to find silence and thinking time. What is it that you need? What things are you drawn to in this season of life? What types of music fill your needs? Who do you love to spend time with, if anyone? Are there places that mend your heart? Activities? Books? TV shows? Begin writing a list of these in your art journal.

Your needs might be less specific, and they might be concepts, like love, or a hug, grace or peace. It might be a good idea to write specific activities or things that resonate with these concepts, so you have something to actively do to fill your needs in that moment. Next take a blank sheet of typing paper and cut strips vertically for a "Take One" flyer. Think about what things you might need to help you survive. Write them down on the strips, and pull one as often as you need.

♥ SELF-CARE

Step outside and collect some pine cones, or dry leaves, twigs, rocks, stones, whatever might be in your surroundings. You might have access to roses. Dried roses are just as beautiful as fresh ones. Create a nature mandala with your findings. You could bring them inside if it's too cold to do this outside. Let this mandala be the release of any anxiety or fear you might have toward the holiday season. Embrace this as an opportunity to generate courage within yourself. You might not feel the joy, or the merriness of it all, but you will survive.

My healing might include laughter, tears, throwing something, creating something, talking, not talking. In other words, it will be as unique as my fingerprints and DNA. And my grieving process will be as predictable as the weather - a completely frustrating mystery.

FACETS OF GRIEF© ▼ *A creative approach to grief*

The Self-Care Plan

Art Therapy Prompt 32

There is something magical that happens when you make the intangible take form, take life, have substance. It becomes more than a fantastical idea. It becomes more than a hope or a wish. It breathes and bleeds, like you do. Put your self-care at the top of your list. I will begin with what self-care isn't. Self-care isn't spending loads of money at a spa or getting wrapped in seaweed or smelling like cucumbers, unless you're into that and can afford that on a whim. Self-care is practical. Scheduling much needed and procrastinated doctor visits, tracking down the supplements your body might need, going on a walk, taking a yoga class or practicing a few minutes in your own home, setting time for quiet time and prayer, meditating, unwinding with Netflix, speaking truths that you've been withholding, retreating to your living room with a good book, making soup, asking for help, ordering take out and on it goes.

More importantly, self-care isn't selfish. The entire purpose of healing is to be able to do more than exist. You want to live, and breathe and do more than survive at some point. It might still feel impossible, and if it does that is okay too. But don't shun the idea that you can do more than survive. Survival becomes a weary place to dwell, that is never how we were intended to live this precious life. Life is rich, and brutal, beautiful and a beast. It is what makes it so impossibly precious.

You can't give, do or think what isn't already in you. If you're running on empty, you can't be expected to show up to a social function ready to engage like your world didn't just implode. Or like you're not living the aftermath every single day. Give yourself grace, gumption, courage to put yourself first this moment.

♡♡ APPLICATION

It might feel ridiculous to write a self-care plan, but don't let that stop you. You can feel free to print this next page out, as many times as you need to. Fill the spaces in, erase things, add things as you go through life. Date them your self-care plan to gauge your grief and progress. Things that help you today might not be serving you tomorrow. Be okay with change. Change is the only constant in life.

☼ SELF-CARE

Brain dump your feelings into the journaling pages below for a minimum of five minutes. Set a timer and don't stop to reread, edit or erase. Play music that helps you clear your head and inspires you to write. YouTube has some great soundtrack music.

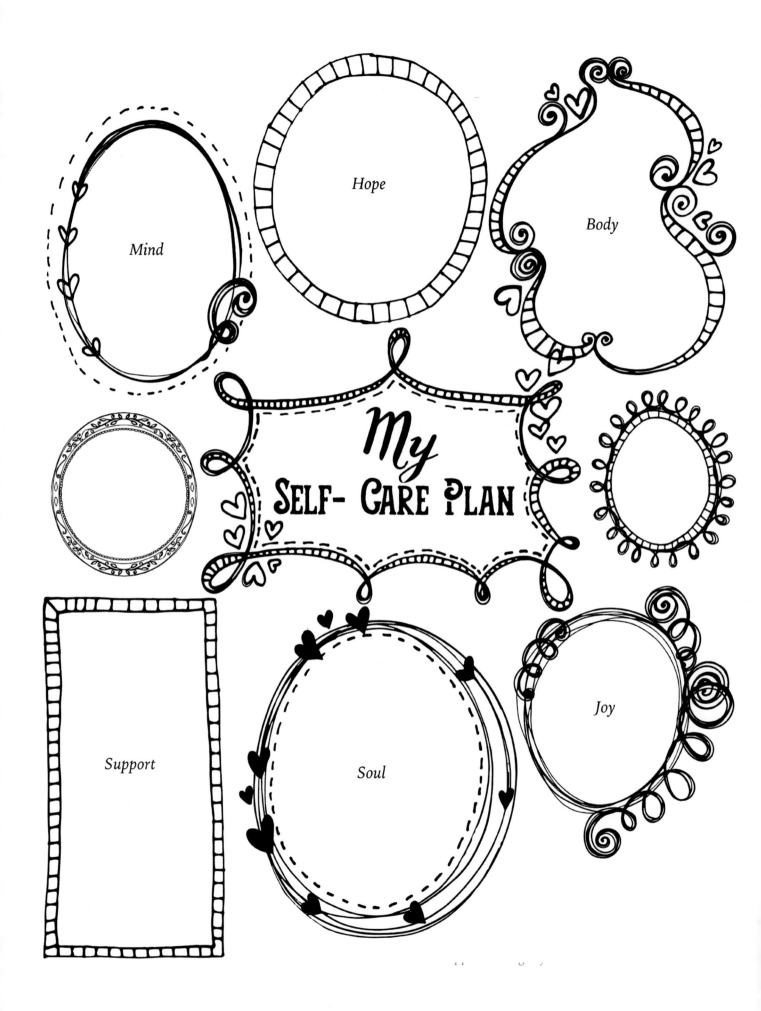

Mind

Hope

Body

My
Self- Care Plan

Support

Soul

Joy

Even when it made no sense at all, she ran with hope. The sadness never left, the loss never became any less painful. But this light after so much darkness was becoming harder and harder to resist.

....

....

....

....

....

....

....

....

....

....

....

....

....

....

....

....

....

....

FACETS OF GRIEF© ▼ *A creative approach to grief*

FACETS OF GRIEF© ▼ *A creative approach to grief*

A Little Wonder

Art Therapy Prompt 33

I don't know when it happened, or how but after a few years of hard, intense, and unrelenting grief, something happened. I hit rock bottom. Emotionally, spiritually and physically exhaustion set in. It's not that I did or didn't **want** to be in heavy grief anymore, it's frankly that I **couldn't**. And somewhere along the way my heart was convinced of this and I let it go. I removed this heavy, worn and unforgiving cloak and cast it away, though it felt more like I was tearing it off, piece by piece, because it hardly fell away easily.

That's not to say I don't have really bad moments, or painful memories. Grief is a lifelong. But the raw and intensity of grief has been replaced with mostly wonder. I wonder a lot and I wonder all the time. About everything. Our family dynamics, our marriage relationship, siblings, birthdays, Thanksgiving, the Saturday morning shenanigans that should include an eldest sister, and the list could go on forever and ever.

The wonder gives me something to do for her. It's my way of spending time with her, not intentionally, but it just happens. Sometimes it's painful but mostly it's a beautiful way her life touches me daily. When the intensity of grief began to fall away I started to feel alive again, like tiny slivers of bright light beaming into this dark hole in the ground. Passions were rekindled like traveling the world someday and learning for the sake of learning. That moment was a big one for me, because when Jenna died I felt like I did too. Proving myself wrong, that part of me that was convinced I didn't need or desire passions and dreams anymore was inaccurate and temporary at most. It was okay to feel and **boy, did it feel good**. I have never felt freer in my life.

♡ APPLICATION

Do you feel wonder in your grief? Or do you feel like you are still caught in the heaviness of it all? There is no short cut through grief. You will do the work for a lifetime, but that doesn't mean life can't be filled with a bit of wonder, dreaming and rekindled or new passions.

What are you drawn to? Is there anything new you feel drawn to? Or is it something from before loss that has rekindled it's appeal to you, even a little? Consider acting on it, do something that involves this wonder, and crave for life. Let the guilt, the sadness, the pain subside. It might feel like betrayal to your child in the beginning, but nothing could be further from the truth. You do not owe anyone a lifetime of misery - that accomplishes nothing. Nothing could be more powerful and meaningful than a lifetime of love dedicated to your child. If you struggle with acting on your wonder and passion, rest assured your grief will be waiting for you when you are through it is up to you to carry it around longer than your heart needs you to. Ask someone you trust to tag along with you on this adventure. Make yourself accountable for enjoying your life again. Step by step by step.

Listen to your grief. Walk with it, and be okay with taking this cloak off.

♡ SELF-CARE

Carve out time to do something new or old. Something adventurous, wild, maybe even fun.
You deserve to laugh, and feel unbroken again.

And then one day, she stopped asking why. She realized no reason following that question could ever be good enough. And while the why's faded in significance, she never stopped wondering who her child would have been.

....

....

....

....

....

....

....

....

....

....

....

....

....

....

....

....

....

....

....

FACETS OF GRIEF© ▼ *A creative approach to grief*

··

··

··

··

··

··

··

··

··

··

··

··

··

··

··

··

··

··

FACETS OF GRIEF© ▼ *A creative approach to grief*

I am

Art Therapy Prompt 34

When you lose a child, it is nearly impossible to resonate with any identity that is not tangled in grief, loss or pain - and for good reason. There are a hundred good reasons not to identify with other things we once were. They hurt to think about, maybe stir up painful memories and others feel like they belonged to another person altogether. Mostly, everything feels senseless after losing a child.

What identities or attributes can you comfortably resonate with? Is your identity still very in tune with your grief? This isn't a good or bad thing, it just is. Own it, make yourself wildly aware of it. Be cautious not to grow comfortable where personal growth could shed light into the dark world of grief.

Think about different areas you could possibly resonate with: your attributes and personality traits, family and friend connections, desires, passions, wounds, healing, spirituality, accomplishments, interests, and on it goes!

Begin a chart in your art journal. Write the identities under each category that you include in your I am chart. For example under the "Family and Friend Connections" you might include mother, daughter, aunt, best friend, etc... in "your passions" you might talk about things that - as we've discussed before - aren't making your world worse. Divide the sections as you feel led, and begin filling it up. You might be surprised how this turns out. This is just an example of one. You are so much more than your grief. You might not feel it, and that is okay. Be patient with yourself.

You could take this one step further and create a silhouette, or use the one on the following page. Shine a spotlight on a large sheet of paper in a dark room to ask someone to trace your silhouette. Divide the silhouette using various colored markers and create your *I am* collage using the things you wrote in each section from your chart.

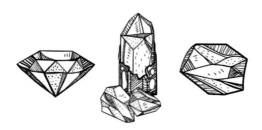

♥ SELF-CARE

Escape somewhere for a few days. Take a drive. Politely decline an invitation. It's okay to not be everything for everyone, especially in grief.

The danger of surviving something so catastrophic is that you ride on this cloud of invincibility. You throw caution to the win, because you often have very little or nothing to lose. Your child died, and you swore with their last breath you'd live full enough for the both of you.

FACETS OF GRIEF© ▼ *A creative approach to grief*

....

....

....

....

....

....

....

....

....

....

....

....

....

....

....

....

....

....

....

FACETS OF GRIEF© ▼ *A creative approach to grief*

Mandalas

Art Therapy Prompt 35

I am drawn to things like dream catchers and mandalas because they illustrate things that sometimes transcend the human language. Tangible things like the feathers on a dream catcher and the lines and curves of a mandala put anger and trust, and brokenness and forgiveness, and emptiness and being spiritually wounded into a format some of us can relate to, more than words. Have you ever drawn or colored a mandala? Consider that it represents some of these: healing, insight, comfort, unity, self-awareness, self-care, balance, harmony, among other things.

The mandala symmetrical, but do not have to be perfect, especially hand drawn ones. The mandala has eight sides, and can include all variations of lines: curved, wavy, straight, rounded and textured.

While the mandala has spiritual roots, I like to think of it as another tool in this universe to use to take decisive action in our own healing. It might be half a step, a baby step or a leap. It might just get you through the next five minutes or hour. But actively, and consciously taking part in your healing is more important that you can even realize if you are in the thick of grief.

♡♡ APPLICATION

In your art journal you might try to draw your own mandala. Surprisingly, it isn't as hard as it might seem. A hand drawn mandala does NOT have to be perfectly symmetrical. It doesn't even have to have eight sides, but this can be helpful to make things even. Here are a few steps to get started:

1. Draw a small circle. Think of it as a compass. Add triangles that point to North, South, East and West
2. Add triangle points in between North, South, East and West. Now you've got 8 spaces to play with… these are your 8 Slices Of Pie.
3. Add a circle to the end of each triangle. Begin adding various shapes and lines on each end.
4. Keep building it. Every time you add something to your Mandala, add it to each of the 8 Slices Of Pie. You can add circles, domes, triangles, squares, lines, waves and outlines and play with different ways of doing circles, domes, triangles, squares, lines, waves and outlines. You can also make up secret symbols, totally break the rules or do anything else you want to do – it's *your* Mandala.

Take a few breaths, and slowly open your eyes to the mandala. Spend a few moments taking in the designs, the lines, the curves, the intricate details. Question yourself, what drew you to this particular design among the others? Let your mind wander. When you are ready, color away. Break as you need to.

♡* SELF-CARE

Consider choosing a word for this year (or month), even if you're half way through it. It might be a word to help you survive, it might be a word that gives you hope, or that comforts you through a dark time. It might be an empowering word, a liberating word… What will your word be? What have your words been in the past?

She was not strong. She was valiant. Radiant. Brave. Broken. The beauty she discovered in the aftermath was unparalleled with anything she had known before, because it had come at such a cost.

FACETS OF GRIEF© ▼ *A creative approach to grief*

The Good, the Random and the Ugly

ART THERAPY PROMPT 36

I don't know if it has more to do with distraction than it does healing, but in the years that followed our daughter's death something that helped subside the vicious cycle of grief was giving back. It felt entirely backwards, but then again nothing made sense about life anymore so that wasn't something I wrestled with much. I went with it.

I had a little blog ages ago and I had an idea, and was lost for words when my readers jumped on board. One of the most precious things I owned while Jenna was in the NICU was a fuchsia journal my mom brought me one day. I asked visitors to write her letters and wrote pieces of our days in it too. When she died I wept over those letters, but it brought me an immense amount of comfort to know how much she was loved and wanted. So I did a "Jenna Journal Drive". Worldwide, people sent journals to me, and altogether we collected almost 900 of them, which we then donated to the hospital she stayed at. That number still sounds crazy to me!

I have to be honest though. There was a high and there was a low to all of this. The high was receiving the journals, the tremendous response, seeing **good** being done in her name. Something good stemming from our tragedy and loss. People thinking about Jenna, mentioning her, using her beautiful name. The low came afterward, almost like a grief hangover.

We did something "big" on her birthday for about 4 years. Each time I did something "big" I realized no amount of journals or good deeds would take away this pain or give us our girl back. Those big things helped though and they served a purpose bigger than me. I needed to do something big those years, and so I did. Rubbing shoulders with death made me fearless, and I have to say that a sense of fearlessness has remained. This invincibility gave me wings to soar, mostly on the courage I saw in that tiny one pound, one ounce baby. If she could fight her fight for 13 days, and face death with so much courage and tenacity, I could do almost anything.

Since those first few years have passed, the grand gestures have become little Random Acts of Kindness like buying someone's coffee or parking cost at the hospital. These smallish things resonate more with where I am at in my grief these days. What does your heart need? Do you need to do something big and momentous? Do you prefer to keep your moments small and inconspicuous? There is no right or wrong, but it helps to define what your heart needs, and be okay with how different those needs are from month to month and year to year.

FACETS OF GRIEF© ▼ *A creative approach to grief*

♡♡ APPLICATION

Have you ever done Random Acts of Kindness in your child's honor? How has it affected you?

Consider planning one, or keep some spare cash with you to pay it forward in your child's name. You can choose to share why you're "paying it forward" or you can keep it anonymous. You can create a hashtag and ask people to join you on a special day through social media. Maybe the biggest gift of all is the gift of distraction from the throbbing pain of grief.

♡ SELF-CARE

Find a good, nourishing recipe and prepare it from start to finish. Find a recipe that sounds good and nourishing to you. Allow yourself to enjoy the process of making something nourishing for your body.

Her memories were her treasures, her source of power, joy and love.

....

....

....

....

....

....

....

....

....

....

....

....

....

....

....

....

....

....

....

....

....

....

....

....

....

....

....

....

....

....

....

....

....

....

....

....

....

....

FACETS OF GRIEF© ▼ *A creative approach to grief*

Choosing Your After

ART THERAPY PROMPT 37

The first few years that followed our daughter's death felt like an out of body experience. I felt things I never knew were possible, I said things I couldn't believe were tumbling out of my mouth, I was becoming an entirely new person and didn't even know it. The first few years were like learning to walk again, learning to breathe, learning to live without hope or passion and very little effort for much else. It was strenuous to do the littlest things like small talk and engage in pregnancy or parenting conversations. My stories were similar, but also couldn't be more different. Living was strenuous. Anything above the essentials was impossible to even think about doing.

I never ever imagined there would be a day that grief wouldn't feel so heavy, so impossible, so permanent, so cruel. So very *in-my-face*.

And while grief is still all of those things, in my own life they are not so *in-my-face* anymore. We are but pawns in this big, messy mystery of life. I don't know how or why, only that enough was enough one day. I got entirely fed up with the sadness. I got angry for a good long while. Unapologetically angry. I wrote a lot. I took up yoga. I swore. I learned to cook nutrient dense food. I learned to pray again. I learned to embrace my own physical strength as a woman again.

Loss paralyzed me. It held me captive in limbo for years. Sometimes in tsunamis of depression and sadness, and other times hail storms of anger and confusion, and rightfully so. In some ways, I still feel captive. It's a captivity I have surrendered to. Captive to endless wonder. I wonder all the time, and about every little way she would have rocked our world.

I have to believe grief, as with any emotion in life has to live out it's full potential. It has a life span. And because grief is a reflection of love, like love, it grows. It has the capacity to throw you into an abyss that will make you feel more alone than you've ever been in your life. It also has a wild and unpredictable capacity to grow.

And that's okay too. I hope if you can't see that today, that you'll take my word for it, that grief cannot be trusted. She has many, many faces. You might feel captured by her dark and relentless waves today, but I hope that one day you get the opportunity to experience her capacity for fearless living.

Grief used to feel a lot like fear. When you learn to take control, you flip it on it's head and it makes you fearless about things you used to have reservations about. You begin to wear your grief like a badge. And you remember any time fear about anything else strikes, that you've endured much, *much* worse. It can't get much worse than losing a child.

So you pace yourself. And you take more deep breaths than a master yoga instructor daily. And you learn to live vibrantly in your own way. One minute, one baby step, one deep breath at a time.

FACETS OF GRIEF© ▼ *A creative approach to grief*

♡♡APPLICATION

It takes courage to even consider doing anything outside of the essentials after losing a child. This might not be something you feel ready for, so as always in grief and especially in this workbook, listen to your heart. Consider writing a bucket list on Life After Loss.

Your bucket list might be to dabble with watercolors again. Pick up your manuscript. Roll out your yoga mat. Lace up your tennis shoes. Train for a marathon or run. Pick up the phone. Jump out of an airplane. Drink more water. Enroll in a class or two. Learn a language.

Your passions might have changed dramatically after loss, as they did for me. And then again maybe some have been rekindled. Go with it, whatever it might be that is calling to you. It might be new territory. Write a list. It might just be one thing. Even if your list includes nothing more than the word BREATHE, write it. Own it. Cherish it. Do it.

Your list is for no one else but *you*.

 ## SELF-CARE

Rest. Find a space, a time throughout your day to rest. Give yourself some time to collect yourself, gather your thoughts, reevaluate your direction and listen to your heart.

....

....

....

....

....

....

....

....

....

....

....

....

....

....

....

....

....

....

....

....

....

FACETS OF GRIEF© ▼ *A creative approach to grief*

FACETS OF GRIEF© ▼ *A creative approach to grief*

....

....

....

....

....

....

....

....

....

....

....

....

....

....

....

....

....

....

....

....

FACETS OF GRIEF© ▼ *A creative approach to grief*

....

....

....

....

....

....

....

....

....

....

....

....

....

....

....

....

....

....

....

....

....

FACETS OF GRIEF© ▼ *A creative approach to grief*

··

··

··

··

··

··

··

··

··

··

··

··

··

··

··

··

··

··

··

··

FACETS OF GRIEF© ▼ *A creative approach to grief*

Dear Grieving Mama,

Firstly, I am profoundly sorry your incredible loss. Thank you for taking part in the Facets of Grief creative workbook. Whether you read through them, did a few of the prompts or all of them, my hope is that you gained something to help you navigate your grief. As a recipient of my creative workbook, you also have access to the online workshop, which includes these workshops and bonus materials such as yoga classes and more coloring pages. To access the bonus material and online workshop please visit the website below:

www.facetsofgrief.com/discover
Password: facetsofgriefbook

My heart is with you.

Sincerely,

Franchesca Cox

Made in the USA
San Bernardino, CA
26 June 2019